CANCELLED

All you need to know about Loft Conversions

All you need to know about
Loft Conversions
by Bill Eykyn

Collins · Glasgow and London

Author's note

It would be difficult to write a book of this sort without the help and co-operation of many people.

Without the support and encouragement of Eileen Lennon and particularly her good humour over hours of dictation and typing, the book might never have seen the light of day. Without the surveying and design expertise of Peter Dell of Attica (Building & Construction) Ltd., the case histories would never have been built, nor would the diagrams and plans have been produced without the efforts of David Smith.

I am most grateful to Jack Smith, C.Eng., F.I.Struct.E., of Angus Smith & Partners, and Vernon A. Hooper, M.I.B.C.O., F.I.A.S., Chief Building Surveyor of the London Borough of Hounslow and Secretary of the Greater London Building Surveyors' Association, for their contributions to the presentation of the technical data and help over the various regulations.

I am indebted to Brian Elsdon, B.Sc. (Hons) for the meat of the final chapter.

My thanks go also to Brock for taking the photographs and to those clients who allowed him into their homes.

First published 1975
Published by William Collins
Sons and Company Limited,
Glasgow and London
Designed and edited by
Berkeley Publishers Limited
© J. W. W. Eykyn 1975
Printed and bound in Spain by
E. Belgas, S. L. Ntra. Sra. de la
Cabeza, 2 - Bilbao. Spain
ISBN 0 00 435484 2

Contents

Introduction

House prices have gone through the roof! It really is from that simple statement of fact that loft conversions have become so important. If a family needs more room there are really only three ways of achieving it: buying a larger house, building a ground floor extension on the existing house, or converting the loft for extra accommodation.

BUYING A NEW HOUSE

Houses are generally categorized by the number of bedrooms they have. An estate agent refers to 'a three-bedroom house' or 'a four-bedroom house'. The amount of living accommodation and the general amenities, while they are important, are of secondary importance when summarizing the status of a property. While priorities can be placed on the size of a living room, the way a kitchen is kitted-out, whether the property has a single or double garage, etc, the first consideration is the number of bedrooms that are available. If a family needs to have four bedrooms, then there is no point in looking at a three bed-roomed house – unless you convert the loft!

Buying a new house not only entails money, it also entails all the performance of actually moving. A change in location can also mean a change of schools and all the costs associated with that. But nowadays it's not just finding the new house, it is also a question of finding a buyer for your present house. The result is that more and more people are now trying to expand their own homes to cater for their expanding families.

GROUND FLOOR EXTENSION

A ground floor extension is fine for creating extra living accommodation such as a study or sun-room or for enlarging a dining room, kitchen, etc. It is not so practical for an extra bedroom or bathroom, if all the sleeping is done on the first floor.

A ground floor extension eats into the garden. This in itself is a disadvantage, which is why the majority of ground extensions are for sun-rooms, conservatories, or for extending the living room with french windows on to a patio. Other common additions are the creation of utility rooms off the kitchen for washing machines, deep freezers, etc. But unless you live in a bungalow, an extra ground floor bedroom is not very convenient.

To gain additional bedrooms is, therefore, a difficult problem. Unless one can build over a garage on the side of the house, there is little alternative to building up a two-storey extension and this, of course, is quite an expensive exercise.

LOFT CONVERSION

A loft conversion is, therefore, a very attractive alternative to moving. In most cases it allows the house to be expanded within itself without encroaching on the land around.

Apart from anything else an empty loft is actually a waste of space and can usually be put into commission without all the performance of planning permission. And in this day and age of red tape and bureaucracy that is quite an important point. It means that you can plan ahead with confidence knowing that your time and money is not being wasted. There is nothing more heartbreaking than to commission a scheme (for which you must pay the design costs) which is going to be turned down by a planning committee because, for example, 'it affects the visual amenity of the area'. Just try and beat *that* phrase on an appeal!

A ground floor extension is relatively easy to conceive but a loft conversion always needs a considerable amount of imagination. When you first clamber into a dirty, gloomy loft and step gingerly from ceiling joist to ceiling joist it is often difficult to appreciate what can be achieved. But when it is all finished, and what was going to be an extra bedroom for the children turns out to be a master bedroom and bathroom for you and your wife, with a small balcony to take the morning air, you will feel the whole thing was worth while. It is just the extension on the mortgage that will make you wince – but that would have happened if you had bought the house you couldn't afford, plus paying for the removal fees, change of school, new curtains, and the rest.

Chapter I
Your loft

Unless you live in a castle, church or some other baronial hall, your house will fall into any one of three main categories. These categories are determined by the shape of the main roof structure as it is positioned on the brickwork forming the perimeter of the house. You will see from the diagrams below that a house usually has either a gable end or a hip, or has a combination of the two, whether it is a detached house, semi-detached or terraced.

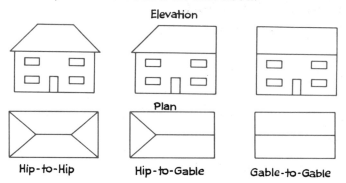

Elevation

Plan

Hip-to-Hip   Hip-to-Gable   Gable-to-Gable

Many houses, of course, have bonnets in the roof as design features. Some have extensions to the rear so that the roof appears L shaped or T shaped. Chimneys can be anywhere around the outside of the house, or come up centrally through the roof. Skylights, with shafts, can obstruct a roof as the light is brought down on to a landing. All these aspects make houses look different and often, from within the roof itself, can look confusing when trying to assess the characteristics of your particular roof space.

HIP-TO-HIP

These are usually detached houses and often have bonnets projecting from them – possibly over a porch or bay window. The larger ones, instead of having a ridge, sometimes have a central flat roof.

HIP-TO-GABLE

Roofs of this type are most often seen on a semi-detached house or at the end of a terraced row of houses.

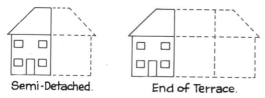

Semi-Detached.   End of Terrace.

GABLE-TO-GABLE

Most terraced houses have a gable-to-gable roof, but of course examples can be seen on detached and semi-detached houses.

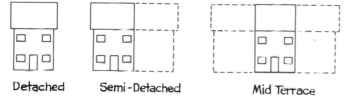

Detached   Semi-Detached   Mid Terrace

CENTRE VALLEY AND OTHER ROOFS

There are other roofs such as a centre-valley roof – often seen on terraced houses in London built during the late Victorian or Edwardian period.

Centre-Valley Roof.

There is the mansard roof, which is basically flat-topped with steeply pitched sides; a completely flat roof; a conical roof – such as the Kentish oasthouses and several other charming variations. But the vast majority fall into the three main categories, with the centre valley and mansard seen quite frequently. The main categories share one common factor vital to the success or otherwise of a loft conversion from within the roof space – the ridge board.

THE RIDGE

The ridge is the most important single factor when considering a loft conversion. It is the height and length of the ridge that determines the headroom that can be made available by dormers being struck out. The height dictates whether it is feasible at all (from within the roof) and the length whether it is worthwhile.

The ridge of the roof has a particular significance in terms of planning permission, as will be seen later. It is also of importance when it comes to cost because if you cannot convert within the roof either the ridge must be raised or, literally, a new roof must be put on, as in the case of a centre valley roof.

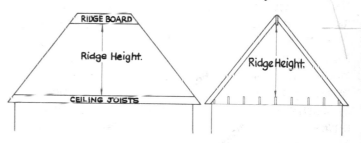

So the first question to be answered is *What is the ridge height*? The measurement is taken from the base of the ridge board to the ceiling joists that you will be standing on in the loft. You will sometimes find bracings and ties that run across the ceiling joists (known as binders) and you will get a false reading if you include them. If the joists are boarded over make allowance for that, too.

Obviously, it is common sense for anyone to see that if the height is only 4 ft (1·2 m) no conversion is possible, contained *within* the roof – unless you and your family are in the Guinness Book of Records as the dwarfs of all time. But even if you were the Tiny Tot of them all, it would not do you any good because the law demands that a certain proportion of the finished floor-to-ceiling height of the conversion is not less than 7 ft 7 ins (or, for the more 'Common Market' minded, 2·3 metres). Incidentally, the regulations used to be 7 ft 6 ins but when the men from the Ministry decided to go metric the figure became 2·3 metres and, when this figure of 2·3 metres is converted back again to feet and inches, it ends up virtually 7 ft 7 ins. The result of this brilliant piece of bureaucracy is that thousands of houses cannot now have a legal habitable conversion. (A store room can be any height.)

At the time the ridge is measured – which, of course, is very early on in your preliminary investigation into the feasibility of a conversion – it is not always possible to determine the size of the *new* floor joists, nor the size of the collars for the dormer.

But, allowing for the thickness of the plasterboard on the new ceiling and flooring on the new joists, you should consider any ridge height measurement under 8 ft 7 ins (2·6 m) as being suspect.

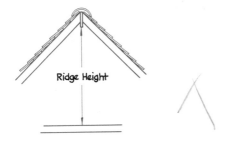

Ideally a ridge height well in excess of 8 ft 7 ins (2·6 m) is desirable to achieve good roof stability without special bracings and beams.

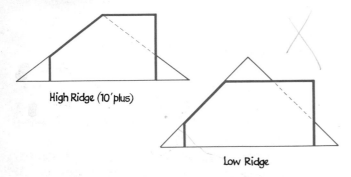

A low ridge height demands additional strengthening at the ridge. So, if you have a low ridge height, be careful in appraising your initial study and read the chapter on 'Designing the Conversion' with particular attention.

If the ridge height is fundamental to the feasibility of converting the loft at all, then it is the length of the ridge that dictates

whether a conversion is a viable proposition or not. It is the ridge length that determines the size of the dormers to the front and/or rear of the property and whether or not a dormer will be possible in the hip of the house.

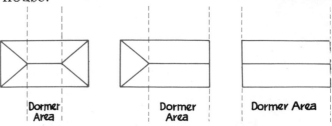

Obviously, a gable-to-gable house is the best property to convert and a hip-to-hip property the worst. Where hipped properties are concerned, the height of the ridge will determine whether a dormer can go into the hip or not, and this is important when assessing the position of the staircase, if it must rise under the hip. This is very often a problem with semi-detached houses in which the existing staircase runs up against the outside flank wall (directly under the hip of the house), but more of this later.

FLOOR AREA

Having established that you have a good ridge height with a decent length to give you proper headroom, the next question is to see what sort of floor area is available.

Here again the shape of the existing roof determines the *usable* floor area. The word *usable* is important: while you do not have to be able to stand everywhere for the floor area to have value, you cannot reasonably be crouching in the eves of the roof and call the floor area there usable.

Generally speaking a height of much less than 3 ft 6 ins (1·07 m) is pretty worthless except for storage. On most roofs this height is also the minimum measurement needed to get proper support for the roof. You will notice that most purlin beams (which run around a roof tying in the rafters) run at a height of about 4 ft (1·2 m).

If you mark a height of 3 ft 6 ins (1·07 m) on two rafters opposite each other and cast your tape between, you will get the approximate measurement of the floor in that direction. Do likewise in the other direction and you will have the overall measurements.

Hip-to-Hip   Hip-to-Gable   Gable-to-Gable

Once again you will see the advantage that a gable-to-gable house has over a hipped one. You can not only achieve more usable floor area at 3 ft 6 ins (1·07 m) but when one adds in the maximum dormer (due to the ridge length) a great deal more headroom at 7 ft 7 ins (2·3 m) is also achieved.

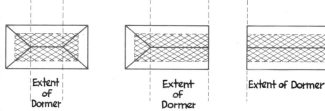

Extent of Dormer   Extent of Dormer   Extent of Dormer

While it is quite reasonable to have dormers in the hip of the roof, they are generally only considered when dealing with a staircase since, in most peoples' eyes, they are not so attractive on the outside. Most hips are on the side elevation of a house and so the usual view of them is from the front or rear of the property where, of course, only the cheek is seen.

If you have a fairly straightforward house that does not have a mass of valleys and bonnets coming into the main roof (and depending on whether you read this sort of book from page one straight through, or whether you skip-read and jump about or not), you will now be feeling excited by the conviction that your loft is probably convertible. By now you can have established whether or not you will have enough ridge height and length and the usable floor area available. But before you shout 'Eureka' there is no point in having a splendid conversion if you cannot get into it!

Unless you want to do the Indian rope trick or have some other Tarzan type approach, you have got only two options: a fixed staircase or a removeable loft ladder. The former gets very technical and the Building Regulations demand all sorts of highly sensible constraints about the angle at which it can rise, the sort of balustrading it has, etc. While the latter is very easy to deal with it is not really on if the conversion is to be part of the house – rather than an extra room stuck up in the loft.

This is why I have devoted a whole section to staircases in this book. At this stage, it is enough to say that if you can see in your mind's eye that the staircase can follow over the existing stairs, fair enough. But will it arrive under a slope of the roof or where a dormer will be? Or could you slice a bit off one of the rooms on the first floor and get up that way? If you just can't see where it can go turn straight to the section on staircases and then – well, either you will feel happier or decide to defer the whole thing until a more expert eye can be brought to bear. Or you might consider a loft ladder as an alternative or abandon the whole project and give this book away as a Christmas present!

The access for the stairs can be very difficult and as often as not cannot be finally determined until the house has been properly surveyed and laid out on a drawing board.

SUMMARY

1. There are three main types of house:
   Hip-to-hip
   Hip-to-gable
   Gable-to-gable
2. The ridge height is a vital factor in determining whether a conversion from *within* the roof is possible or not – a finished floor-to-ceiling height of 7 ft 7 ins (2·3 m) must be achieved.
3. The ridge length governs the width of dormers and the overall head room at full height.
4. Is the conversion worthwhile?
   The measurement at the plane of 3 ft 6 ins (1·07 m) determines the usable floor space.
5. Consider where the staircase can most logically be fitted. If it looks tricky you may have to wait until the house is surveyed and an assessment made from the drawing board.

Chapter II

Your local planning authority

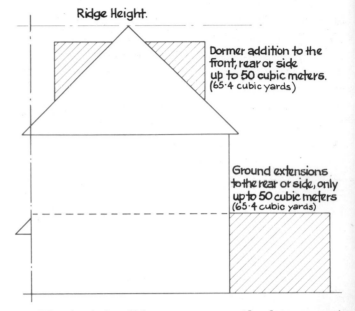

Ridge Height.

Dormer addition to the front, rear or side up to 50 cubic meters. (65·4 cubic yards)

Ground extensions to the rear or side, only up to 50 cubic meters (65·4 cubic yards)

T his is where we take a walk along the corridors of power. This is where the politics start. This is often considered the land of *who* you know, not *what* you know.

'Tis a gloomy business is planning permission. Full of black clouds and drizzle. But every cloud has its silver lining and in this case it is called 'permitted development'.

PERMITTED DEVELOPMENT

A few moons ago, when they enacted the Town and Country Planning Act, it was decided that some development to a property could be undertaken without permission from the local planning authority. Under what is known as a General Development Order, Article 3, certain classes of development could be undertaken without the permission of the local planning authority or the Minister.

The different classes cover some odd subjects, such as 'being able to use as a shop for any purpose a tripe shop' or '. . . a cat-meat shop', or 'the painting of the exterior of any building or work otherwise than for the purpose of advertisement, announcement or direction'.

The class *we* are interested in is 'Class I – Development within the curtilage of a dwelling house'. Under this class, you may enlarge your dwelling by up to 1,765 cubic ft (50 cubic metres) or by not more than ten per cent of the original cubic content up to a maximum of 4,061 cubic ft (115 cubic metres), providing you do not exceed the height of the original house or project beyond the forwardmost part of any wall which fronts on a highway.

The 'original' house means the house as it was built or, if it is pre-1948, as it was in 1948. This is, of course, very good news when it comes to a loft conversion within the roof since the empty loft space is counted as part of the 'original' house and it is, therefore, only the dormers projecting from it that count as 'enlargement'.

Part of Original House.

There is a snag (there *has* to be!). The addition of a garage counts as an 'enlargement' to the dwelling and so its cubic capacity must be totted up if it has been added to the house after 1948. But if you have erected some other small building such as a summerhouse or outhouse 'for the keeping of poultry, bees, birds, pet animals or other livestock for the domestic needs or personal enjoyment of the occupants of the dwelling house' it is not treated as the enlargement of the house. You may enjoy the birds and the bees, gratis.

In one case where a garage was falling apart through mis-use, it was taken down and the loft constructed under 'permitted development' and then planning permission granted for the new garage very easily because the property already had 'vehicular access'. But before you dash out with an axe and 'mis-use' your garage, do remember that there is no legal precedence with planning decisions. That was a case where, right or wrong, the *who* not the *what* came in!

Permitted development still holds good in a conservation area, but not on a listed building, or where there is a special order. If you want to be a real masochist just try a loft conversion in the Hampstead Garden Suburb in north London. That was a case where they invoked the next clause, Article 4, entitled 'Directions restricting permitted development'.

Article 4 may be summed up as being the way the Minister or the local planning authority can get off the hook if any particular area is getting a caning from building work carried out under permitted development. By slapping an Article 4 notice on an area all permitted development is stopped, and the long haul of trying to obtain planning permission must be started.

But P.D. (as it is called) is a very useful means for enlarging your home without all the red tape of planning applications. Now you will see why the ridge height is so critical when designing a loft conversion.

A loft conversion is also the only development which can, effectively, come to the front of a house without planning consent. It also means that you can plan your project with safety and you can do it speedily. With building costs rising all the time, if you can avoid three months or more getting a job through planning, you will save yourself both money and aspirins.

Permitted development is very definitely the silver lining of the black cloud which we must now consider for the sake of those who have no alternative.

PLANNING OFFICERS AND COMMITTEES

The working of a local planning authority is, of course, democracy in action. Naturally we feel pleased we have a democratic system and, presumably, local planning authorities. The main problem with democracy can be summed up in a word: politics. It all revolves around the fact that the fifty-one-percent's can overrule the forty-nine-percent's whether they are right or wrong.

While local authorities do have the odd 'Independent', most of them, like the Parliamentary breed, are made up of the 'Con-Lab-Lib' variety of homo sapiens. This can have a very definite bearing on your planning application whether you or they like it or not – because a planning application is you, the individual, asking a whole diverse collection of other individuals if you can do your own individual thing! Well, where do you find these powerful chaps?

First of all, answer the question '*Where do you pay your rates?*' This will tell you who your local planning authority is. Whichever council it is will have a planning committee which will be delegated to deal with your application (it usually has to be a very large scheme for the committee to have to refer it to the whole council before a decision is made). The committee is made up of lay people 'like you and me' and, just because of that, they have all sorts of axes to grind.

Consequently, in some areas you can have an easy ride and in others a rough one. Every committee up and down the country will have its reputation and it is most important that you find out what yours is. Fortunately, there is a very good gentleman to talk to and he is normally very helpful.

THE PLANNING OFFICER

Planning officers are the paid professionals. They are the chaps who really know the ropes. They see committees come and go, they have seen councils change from red to blue and back again. Their lot is a pretty hard one at the best of times but, in the best traditions of the Civil Service, they try to keep out of politics and just *interpret policy*. And nowadays, with the number of applications there are to deal with, they are busy and hard pressed. However, a visit to the town hall and a quick chat about what you have in mind will reap a high dividend.

For a start, your planning officer will tell you exactly what paper work is required (and it is not his fault, remember!) but, more important, he will tell you whether he feels that what you have in mind will be acceptable or not. There may be specific technical grounds for turning the scheme down, which he will soon point out to you, but the main thing is that he will know the committee's views. So don't try and argue the toss with him, because his recommendation goes a long way. The committees *always* listen to the planning officer's recommendation and the vast majority of committees accept them. Remember, he will recommend according to his brief, not because he, as an individual, thinks it is good or bad – although he would not be human if his own feelings had no influence.

If you cannot get the planning officer's approval and you feel that your scheme cannot be compromised, then it will still go before the committee and your only hope is the *who* technique. One only has to look round any area – town or countryside – to see that the only way a particular project got through was because 'someone knew someone' on the planning committee. It also works the other way: quite reasonable schemes have been turned down because an objector has 'known someone who knew someone . . .'

The planning authority must notify neighbours and other interested parties once a scheme is formally submitted, so it is as well to do your own investigations first. Talk to your neighbours. If you can get their blessing in advance it is a great help.

It is quite impossible to give a general guidance on what will or will not be acceptable. As all people are different so are all committees. And they change their minds, so that you cannot even go by a precedent in the same street.

Because the whole thing is political you have the right to appeal to the Minister if your application is turned down. When a rejection is given reasons have to be stated in writing but, before you rush to appeal, consider first whether you can overcome the objections. Very often only a small change would get your plan through. Then the committee refers it back to the planning officers so that if you agree and an amendment can be incorporated, then the application can be referred to the next committee meeting. If they just don't like it you have no alternative but to appeal. But remember, even if you get through on an appeal, the whole performance could cost you a lot of money on the building cost through the time delay. It could be six months or more!

Planning committees meet at monthly intervals – in some of the urban areas twice monthly – but the amount of business they get through varies enormously. They can spend hours on one particular application and rubber-stamp another scheme on the planning officer's recommendation.

Although your application can be on the agenda the committee may not reach that item and it may have to be held over to the next meeting. Nowadays it is not uncommon for applications to take three or four months before you get a decision. This will certainly cost you more money on your building estimate and it can be a very depressing business.

While there are bound to be inefficiencies in any system, the main reason for all the delays is the fact that there has been a substantial and continuing increase in private planning applications with only the same number of people to deal with them. In theory, councils should be pleased to see more development for this is a very real source of income. You may get all the services connected with your application for free, but once it is through and your project built your property will be the subject of a re-valuation and there will be an increase in the rates.

Planning is, indeed, a gloomy business and

the best thing is to get someone else to handle the whole thing for you. The trouble is knowing who – and where to get hold of what sort of outfit to suit your needs best.

DESIGN SERVICES

In this age of mass communication there is that wonderful little instrument the telephone. Nearly everyone has one, which also means that nearly everyone has that state 'book club' best giveaway, the Post Office Telephone Directory. At the back of the Directory we find those pages that help to keep the printing costs down and the weight up. If armed in no other fashion you may start your search with just these two tools.

There are four main types of people who could help you produce the design and drawings that you need: architects, surveyors, designers, and loft conversion specialists. The first three will only design and see your project through up to the building stage, but you will have to employ a building firm to construct the conversion – often, though, under their supervision. Only the latter will give you a packaged deal combining both.

The first two mentioned are main headings in the telephone Yellow Pages. Both belong to professional institutes (to which you can write) and as such do not advertise. You therefore have no idea whether they would be prepared to tackle your scheme or not until you have contacted them. The larger practices would tend to find this type of work uneconomic (or you might find their fees rather a lot!)

Designers cover a multitude of names, such as design consultants, design draughtsmen, architectural designers, design services and the rest and while the Yellow Pages tend to put them under the heading design consultants, you will also find under that heading electronic designers, tracers and a whole variety of activities. You should have one or two amusing phone calls!

The loft conversion specialists have a heading in the index referring them to 'Building Contractors' and under that heading you are bound to see bold advertisements offering their services. I have devoted a section to the role played by the specialist firms later in this book as their expertise needs a more detailed look *after* you have absorbed the greater part of the subject.

The first three types are all perfectly good alternatives in achieving a set of drawings and getting your project through the local authority. Any of the former can also provide the supervision that the project needs when the builders are in action.

However, it is one thing to design it but quite another to get it built – and at a price that can be afforded. And by price one not only means the money expended, but the unquantifiable cost in terms of frustration, fatigue and fear during the course of construction.

Very few architects or surveyors would be interested in making a living out of only designing loft conversions, so that to an architect this sort of work is a 'one off' job. Their higher qualifications are surely put to better use in designing whole houses, offices and factories. And there is a lot of difference in designing commercial projects, where the restrictions on the builder related to access, storage of materials, working conditions etc, are far less than operating a building site on top of a private house with the occupants in residence.

The design consultant who takes on loft conversions may not have the academic qualifications of an architect, but he may well be much more experienced in the practical procedures involved. But whether you use an architect with a string of letters after his name or a design consultant with no qualifications, they will both be much more concerned to please you, the client, who forks out their fees, than pleasing the builder who is asked to tender against their drawings and specifications. Both must have practical building knowledge to do their jobs at all, but you will gain more from the man who has real experience in this field – whatever his pedigree.

By far the best designer to use is the man who has not only had real experience in loft conversion work, but has had to cost the project out, actually get hold of the materials he has specified and been responsible for getting them to site and used. When that man puts ink on the drawing board he really knows what it is all about. He will try and design himself (and you, the client) out of trouble. So often the designer is too far behind the scenes and does not have to follow through the consequences of his own making or face the real problems.

In the next chapter you will see the importance of a sound approach to design, the main points that need to be considered and how they should be dealt with. Standards in drawing work vary wildly but once you have seen good lay-out work and a drawing that details the structural elements properly, you will recognise fairly quickly whether you should place your confidence in a particular outfit or not. A good builder will recognise a decent set of plans; your judgement of the builder will be helped if you, too, know how to judge the competence of the drawings.

SUMMARY

1. If your conversion adds less than 1,765 cubic ft (50 cubic metres), or ten per cent of the 'original' house up to a maximum of 4,061 cubic ft (115 cubic metres), you may build under 'permitted development' provided that:
   You do not exceed the ridge of the house.
   You do not go beyond the forwardmost part of the house.
2. Permitted development holds good in a conservation area but not on a listed property.
3. Any area may be the subject of an Article 4 order restricting permitted development. Check.
4. If planning permission is required go and see the planning officer of your local planning authority (where rates are paid).
5. The planning officer will want to see plans and advise you accordingly. Heed his advice. His recommendation carries a lot of weight. He will tell you how to complete a planning application.
6. If you want someone to handle your application and drawings for you there are four main channels to use:
   Architects
   Surveyors
   Design Consultants
   Loft Conversion Companies.
7. If you use an architect, surveyor or design consultant you will have to employ a firm of builders. Only the loft conversion companies will give you a package deal.
8. In choosing your designer look for real experience, not just qualifications.

Chapter III

Designing the conversion

Having established that your loft conversion is 'on' the next stage is to have your house surveyed and laid out on a drawing board. The surveyor should arrive at your door armed with a six foot (two metre) rule, tape and notebook together with one of those instant print cameras (if he wants to save himself time sketching). If he is really on the ball he will have found out – when making the date with you – whether your loft has a light in it, whether you have a step ladder and will have made sure in advance that he can get into every room in the house. (No point your having locked the study and lost the key!)

The survey will probably take two or three hours and consists in the main of measuring every single room in the house – including, of course, the loft. So if you are nervous that he might steal all the silver should you go out, make sure you are free for the morning or afternoon as the case may be. He won't appreciate your following him around asking a lot of questions, since he needs to concentrate. He will want to ask you questions and, indeed, he will want to hear all you have to say – but in the right order.

Outside the measurements of all and everything, he will be looking into all the constructional aspects and ancillary factors such as:

Load bearing walls
State of all brickwork
Condition of the roof
Positions of chimneys and flues
Condition of electrical wiring
Positions of soil vent pipes
Water tanks and plumbing
Stair access
Positions of windows
Party walls
Zones of open space
Site location
Storage of materials and plant

He will want to determine your prime requirements and discuss alternatives with you where the options are open. At this stage he will want as much information as he can get to lay out the drawing and start originating the design. It will not be until he has the layout drawing that he will want to know the specific features you wish to be incorporated, such as cupboards, style of bathroom suite and staircase design. He will be sure that he can achieve the layout and that some particular structural aspect does not affect the basic design.

The manner in which the jig-saw is put together will be according to his experience. At this stage he must obtain the basic parameters to lay out the drawing and start the real design work. Usually, the major design discussion starts with the layout drawing in hand. Mind you, it is during this first meeting that you will decide one very important thing: have *you* confidence in the man? You will soon know whether you want him to do your job by the way he puts his questions and the way in which he answers yours. Does he appear to be on your wavelength, in tune with your ideas? Can you trust him when he says something can't be done? Is it just that he can't do it, or can it *really* not be done because it is just too impracticable or too costly?

When you and the building society bought the house, it was probably the biggest financial commitment you have ever made. Your loft conversion is likely to be the second. Good heavens, you could buy a very decent second-hand Rolls Royce for the price of many loft conversions and, for some of the larger ones, a brand new one!

With the survey complete and your basic parameters established, the surveyor will then return to his office and start the laborious process of laying out the drawing. Initially, he will lay out the house exactly as it stands now. He will lay out the ground floor and first floor as existing and will produce a layout of the loft – all these as a

plan drawing. He will then produce a section through of the first floor in relationship to the loft and the roof line.

He will now be in a position to establish the load bearing walls of the house. Virtually all the internal walls on the ground floor will be load bearing, but when you get on to the first floor very often the walls are hollow stud partition walls. Often the first floor walls are not necessarily in line with the ground floor and wherever this occurs they will not be load bearing walls. However, where a wall runs right the way through the house – very often, for example, dividing the living room and the dining room on the first floor and the main bedroom and second bedroom and bathroom on the first floor – these walls are load bearing, i.e. they are solid brick running from the top of the house through to the foundations beneath the ground floor.

Load bearing walls are particularly significant when trying to break the spans up in the loft in terms of the structural design. Where a load bearing wall exists this will be shown on the drawing on the plan of the loft conversion as dotted lines and it is only on these walls that the designer can rely when trying to break the spans.

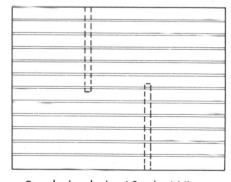

Span broken by Load Bearing Walls.

If the overall span is, say, 20 ft (6·1 m) and there is no load bearing wall then obviously either very large joists must span across unbroken, or steel work will have to be incorporated to break the span. But, if there are load bearing walls running through, of course, the span is automatically broken and joists can bear from both sides. The unbroken spans of the conversion dictate the depth of the joists required and this is important when one is considering the floor-to-ceiling height of the new conversion – especially where there is a low ridge since, of course, the depth of the joists eats into the overall ridge height.

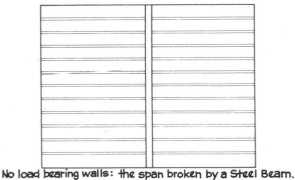

No load bearing walls: the span broken by a Steel Beam.

Load bearing walls are, therefore, a most significant factor in laying out the floor. But the existing loft area will have struts and bracings coming down from the rafters supporting the roof and until all these bracings have been removed the area in the loft will be useless – but, by the same token, the struts and bracings cannot be removed without additional and further supports for the roof.

This is where the designer will incorporate trusses, trussed purlins, or some other means of support and this is usually done at the 3 ft 6 ins (1·07 m) plane of the roof.

Calculations will normally allow proper and safe support at this height and it is merely the most suitable method which has to be considered. Very often steel is used in the form of steel beams to obtain the strength for the loading, but on the other hand large joists bolted together, or large joists with a flitch of steel forming a sandwich, can give the required strength for the floor and the support off this can then be made by way of struts or studding to the rafters. Other factors, such as the size and width of the dormer and its loading on to the trusses, affects the make-up of the supports at this point.

The type of members to be used to gain the support and the actual constructional technique that is to be involved will, of course, very much depend upon the experience of the designer and his knowledge of how the construction is to take place. The size of loft, the working area, the access to it – all these count in terms of the builder being actually able to position the members concerned. It must be appreciated that all these members are inevitably large in order to have the strength required. These members have to be delivered to site and have to be taken up into the loft and it is the feasibility of this that is important, not only in terms of the practical aspects but also in terms of the cost involved.

Once the truss members are located and the floor area established then consideration can be given to the dormers and their size and shape. Once again spans count a lot in terms of the size of the ceiling collars (that is the joists that are used to take the dormer roof). And here again the ridge height is most significant. The closer to the ridge, the more support will be required at the ridge in terms of strength. Given a good ridge height, the stronger the apex of the roof will be in terms of bolting the new ceiling collars to the existing rafters. The width of the dormer will, of course, be determined by the ridge length.

The larger the dormer the greater the headroom available underneath it. Dormers are only created for headroom, and while one will want to have the largest dormers possible from the interior point of view, obviously the outside must be considered in aesthetic terms so that the overall conversion will blend in with the exterior of the house. At this stage the designer is trying to obtain the minimum amount of headroom to produce a decently proportioned room or rooms, as the case may be. It is when he has got his preliminary layout that he can then consider, with you, the size and the proportion of the dormers in relation to the external appearance. Also, it must be remembered that the larger the dormers are and the more required, the greater the cost.

In establishing the floor area and the position of the dormers the designer is looking for two main factors. First, he must achieve a decent floor area after allowing for the staircase access to the room. Second, he must achieve sufficient headroom by way of the dormers so that the room can be a legal habitable size. The law demands that the 7 ft 7 ins headroom must be achieved over an area that is equivalent to half the area at a plane of 5 feet (or, to be precise, its height should not be less than 2·3 metres over an area of the floor of the room equivalent to not less than one half the area of the room measured on a plane in 1·5 metres above the floor).

The basic layout, therefore, must consist of a properly constructed floor with the existing roof adequately supported, the access of the stairway so designed that it can enter the new floor at the correct height and that the room or rooms concerned must have a proper legal height by way of the dormers to be constructed.

After this it is then a question of maximising the space available, bearing in mind the external appearance and the cost involved. Other factors must also be taken into account in terms of the Building Regulations or the Inner London Byelaws – both of which are covered in Chapter V.

DORMERS

Having now established the basic layout and general feasibility of the conversion, the designer will then return to you, drawing in hand, to see whether the basic layout meets your needs. It is at this point that he can then start discussing the dormers with you, their size and outside appearance.

In most cases it is only the dormers that indicate to the outside world that you have had a loft conversion. Their appearance is therefore of paramount importance. Any dormer which has just been 'stuck' on the house will look quite ghastly. A good designer will try to achieve total harmony with the existing lines and appearance of the house.

There are really only two sorts of dormers: a standard dormer set into the roof and a bay dormer which comes to the extremities of the roof (i.e. the outside wall). Wherever possible one should try to achieve the standard dormer since this can be made to blend in with the roof and give the overall appearance that the house was built with its loft already converted. A bay dormer is always a very bulky affair and should only be used where it is essential or where it cannot easily be seen. The advantage of a bay dormer is only appreciated from the increase of room on the inside.

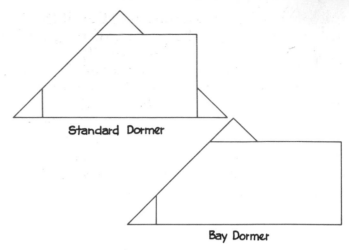

Standard Dormer

Bay Dormer

As the primary function of a dormer is to give headroom, generally speaking nearly all the dormers have flat roofs although they can look very attractive if they are crowned. However, it takes a very high loft to be able to achieve this and, therefore, opportunities to do so are rare. The flat roof of a dormer can either slope forward with a gutter running along the facia, or it can slope backwards draining into a box gutter and then on to the main roof.

Dormer draining into gutter.

Dormer draining back onto main roof.

The cheeks of the dormer are usually tiled – using the existing tiles from the roof so that the age and weathering of the tiles are as much in keeping as possible with the main roof. Some dormers can look very attractive with the cheeks of the dormers finished in facia boarding and it is sometimes pleasant to see white facia boarding contrasting with grey slate. Many people have used Canadian red cedar for the cheeks of the dormer, but this has a disadvantage in that after about a year the cedar boarding tends to 'silver' in colour and then looks rather shabby. Any wood facing, whether it is painted or not, has to be attended to every so often, but where the cheeks of the dormer have either been tiled or slated, maintenance is considerably reduced.

The windows of the dormers are very important in terms of appearance. Generally one tries to use frames similar to those used on the floors below, but this is not always possible. If a house has leaded lights it can look very much more attractive if the dormers also have leaded lights. It is all very much a question of taste and appearance, but it is certainly something to which planning officers pay particular attention, so wherever possible the windows should blend in with the house. If you were to have Georgian windows, then it is unlikely that you would be able to have double glazing. Since double glazing is something which is considered by many people to be important nowadays, very often a house that has Georgian windows will, in fact, not have these windows in the loft conversion but have a traditional range so that they can be double glazed. Cost and delivery also play their part in terms of the style of windows used.

Bay dormers are usually used on the hips of houses to get the stairs up, and are otherwise used to the rear of terraced properties where the appearance is not so pronounced.

Below: A large bay dormer to the rear of the property, clad with shiplay boarding, with french windows opening onto a balcony.

Above: Dormers set neatly into the roof with the cheeks tile-hung to match the existing tiles.

Below: A long standard dormer with leaded lights to match the windows on the floor below.

The bay dormers on the hips are usually tiled, but the bay dormers to the rear of properties are usually built up in brick. A terraced property has the advantage of parapet walls which can be built up and the rear wall can be built up containing the windows with a flat roof extending over the whole area from the ridge.

The covering of the dormers is obviously important since once they are built one certainly wants to keep down the maintenance as much as possible. The traditional covering is three layers of roofing felt with chippings; however there are now special P.V.C. laminate products on the market for the purpose. Providing the product is laid exactly in accordance with the manufacturer's specification there is no reason why a proper watertight finish should not be obtained, but it has to be remembered that it only takes a very small puncture in the surface for a leak to become apparent. Therefore it is advisable to consider asphalt when weathering very large dormers. A properly asphalted roof will stand the test of severe weather over a prolonged period and there is no doubt that if there is a need to get out on to the roof it will withstand much more traffic. If a dormer roof of any size has been asphalted, then you and the builder can sleep in your respective beds at night far more easily!

Dormers can be made to look very attractive and it is certainly an aspect of the conversion that needs close attention to insure that the end result really does marry in well with the house. A rough looking dormer, cheaply finished with zinc sides, is not necessarily any less expensive than a well designed one properly finished. Badly designed dormers usually cause problems and, in the end, cost you more money in terms of sorting out the leaks and defects, as well as presenting a permanent eyesore giving rise to the feeling: 'I wish we had done it properly to start with.'

SLOPING ROOFS

If the ridge height of the loft space is very high, it may be possible to produce a loft conversion without having any dormers at all. In this case the light and ventilation can be achieved through the use of Velux windows. These windows have been specially

Above: A brick-built bay dormer to the rear of the property with the adjoining parapet walls built up and water tanks on the roof.

conceived for the purpose and come in a variety of different sizes.

It is rare for dormers not to be required, but additional light and ventilation can be gained on the side of the roof that does not have a dormer window. The windows are double glazed and have the ability to incorporate a roller blind within the window frame itself.

Because of their pivot action it is easy to reverse the window to clean it and since it fits on the outside of the roof additional headroom – to the value of the depth of the rafters – can be gained internally.

The photograph below shows how useful these windows are for creating additional light and ventilation in what would otherwise be the blind side of the conversion.

Top: Dormers set into the roof on two sides with the cheeks tiled to blend in.

Above: Velux windows set into the roof slope give more light than the equivalent size of standard windows built into a dormer.

STAIRCASES

If it is the dormers that either make or mar the external appearance of a conversion, then it is certainly the staircase that does the same for the internal appearance. Once again, the whole point of the conversion is to give the appearance that it all forms part of the house in a natural way and is not just 'a room up in the loft'. The position and design of the staircase is, therefore, most important and needs particular attention to detail.

Wherever possible the new staircase to the loft should follow over the existing staircase. Not only are you using dead space above the staircase, but it gives the opportunity to design the staircase along exactly the same lines as the existing one. This allows the new floor to blend in naturally with the house.

But staircases are a problem in that they need a certain amount of space and if that space is not available then some part of the house must be lost for the stairs to exist at all. A further complication is the fact that, under the Building Regulations, the staircase has to conform to certain very definite requirements and these, on occasions, can be quite onerous. While the regulations are designed to ensure safety there is no question that there are times when something less than the regulations allow would be perfectly acceptable to you, the owner of the property.

The argument is, of course, that you may not be the permanent owner of the house and that any new occupant might suffer as a result of what you have done. The fact that any new occupant would first of all have to see what you have done and make up his or her mind whether or not to have the house is, of course, a matter for debate. However, it is a debate you cannot hope to win so the short answer is to meet the regulations and to do the best that can be done.

The local authority has power to relax the regulations concerning staircases. Their normal view is that at the time of design it should certainly conform but if during construction certain problems mean that the staircase would technically infringe a certain aspect of the regulations then they would consider giving the relaxation.

There are two important criteria related

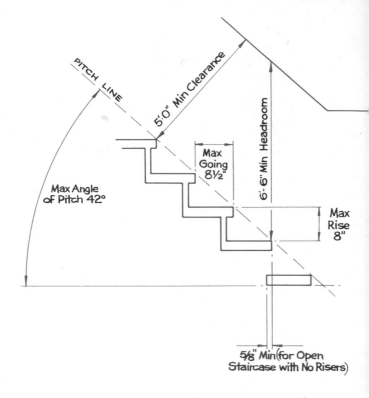

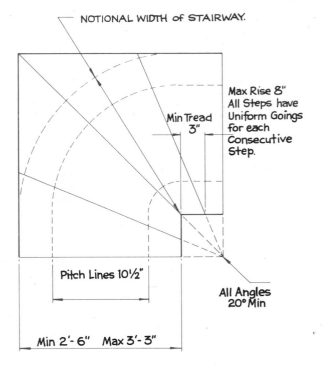

to private stairways and they involve the angle at which the staircase can rise and the minimum headroom over a staircase.

You will see from the diagram (top) that the pitch line cannot exceed an angle of more than 42° and that the minimum headroom from the tread cannot be greater than 6 ft 6 ins (2·0 m). Also the measurement at a right angle from the pitch line (i.e. from the nosing of the tread) must give a minimum clearance of 5 ft (1·5 m).

The rules are further complicated by the fact that each parallel stair must have an equal depth of tread or 'going'. Further regulations come in, if the staircase has winders in it. With the majority of loft conversions space is at a premium and almost every staircase is involved with winders.

Therefore, it is as well to remember that if winders are involved the minimum width of staircase is 2 ft 6 ins (75 cm). A staircase may, on the other hand, have either quarter or half landings. These are preferable in terms of safety and usually in terms of aesthetics, although circumstances will very much dictate that which is feasible.

The style of the staircase is obviously very much up to the individual. Nowadays there is a trend for open plan stairs and admittedly they do bring more light down through the stairwell – especially where they cross a window. But as most staircases usually follow over existing stairs it is more common

to see treads and risers used with the soffit (or underside) of the stairs plastered to match existing decor (see photo page 23).

Very often the side of the staircase should be a 'cut string' but this is more expensive to produce than when the staircase is set into a string.

This is often a point where the pennies are saved. If the existing staircase has a cut string it is a great shame not to follow in the same way. The same goes for the balusters. A lot of the older staircases have turned balusters and so many of the loft converters do not bother to run to turned balusters, but save the cost instead. It really is worth paying particular attention to staircases, because it is the staircase alone that can really make a loft conversion. A badly made staircase can ruin an otherwise perfectly good loft conversion. But in this day of mass production, this is where some of the better refinements get lost – and it is a great shame.

Staircases are often made of soft wood as well as the balustrading, because they are painted before being carpeted. However, the handrail is again a vital ingredient in terms

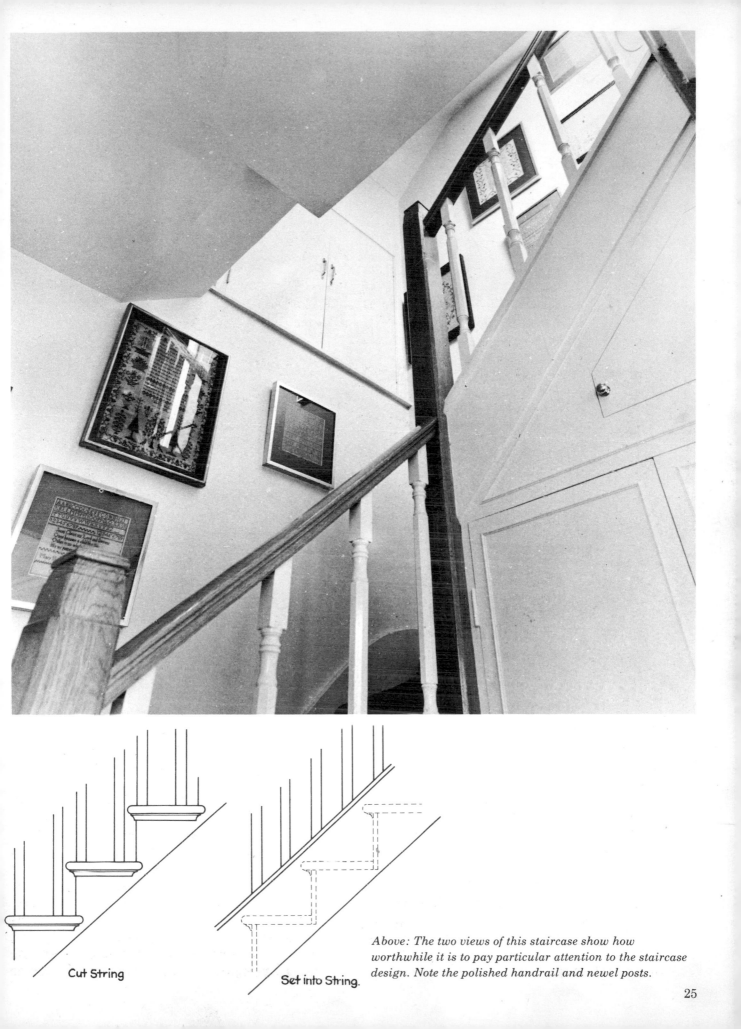

Cut String

Set into String.

Above: The two views of this staircase show how worthwhile it is to pay particular attention to the staircase design. Note the polished handrail and newel posts.

of aesthetic design. A half round mahogany handrail can make a lot of difference to the finished product. Or, if your existing staircase has an oak handrail, it is well worthwhile ensuring that the new one follows in exactly the same way. While hard woods are indeed a good deal more expensive than soft woods, it is certainly not worth spoiling the ship for a ha'porth o' tar! Not with a staircase.

The staircase shown in the photograph on the left shows how worthwhile it is to spend time and trouble designing a staircase properly. If you live in a modern house, by all means have a modern looking staircase. But if you live in an Edwardian or late Victorian house or even in a house built in the thirties, try to follow the lines of your staircase and you will find this is enormously rewarding. It is a potentially expensive part of the project but is so worthwhile getting right.

Colour magazines, 'glossies' and excited journalists often make a great thing out of spiral staircases. Spirals always look fantastic on television sets where the Man at the Top lives in his converted barn and has a magnificent spiral staircase leading up to his boudoir. The television cameras always catch the beautiful legs as they ascend with the man following – just like the original member of the jet set. But when it comes to everyday living by far the greater number of houses that could have a loft conversion could not possibly have a spiral staircase.

The reasons, in fact, are very simple. First, because they are spiral, it is absolute hell to get beds, furniture and everything else up into the new conversion.

Second, because all the weight of the staircase is on the central spindle and this can cause considerable difficulty in terms of erection.

Third, if one allows 2 ft 6 ins (75 cm) on either side of the central spindle, it is easy to see that an overall diameter of 5 ft (1·5 m) is required for the staircase to rise up from the floor below to the new conversion. This means that a considerable amount of floor space has to be devoted to the spiral staircase and, in most houses, this is just not feasible.

Spiral staircases are super – but don't get too excited about having one unless you have a large house and a good size bank account. They waste space and are only realistic if you have the space to waste! If a staircase can follow over an existing staircase then, of course, the dead space above it is being used in a sensible way. If you cannot go over the existing staircase because of the headroom available, then of course you can consider a spiral staircase rising from another room, but don't get carried away with the aesthetic approach if you are trying to keep the costs down.

If no staircase can be built, then the only alternative is to have a loft ladder. There is no doubt that a loft ladder detracts from the overall value of a new conversion in that the new conversion must look like an afterthought rather than blending in with the house. The advantage of a loft ladder is that it does not have to conform to any regulations and can therefore rise as steeply as you, the owner, will permit. If it is possible for you to have a straight ladder – rather like a ship's companionway – this can be made as a very solid structure, *provided* it can be made so that it is removable.

There are many different types of loft ladder available on the market and virtually all of them are practical ways of being able to get from one floor to the other. The cost can be very low and the fitting of them quite simple. But their conventional use is really much more for getting into an empty loft than into a fully-fledged loft conversion.

PLUMBING

Nearly all loft conversions involve a certain amount of plumbing if only to remove the water tank to a fresh position out of the way. Obviously an electrician is needed to give the basic source of power and light and normally a plasterer will give the finished effect before the painting and decorating.

The plumber is often the first man on site. It is rare indeed to find a loft that has the water tanks positioned in exactly the right place for a loft conversion – let alone all the service pipes running to it. The designer, therefore, has to bear in mind when laying out his drawing the most suitable position for the water tanks. It is a relatively simple matter if no plumbing services are required in the new loft conversion. In such a case the tanks merely have to be shifted to a convenient position and the pipes re-routed to allow for the new floor to be laid. However, if the new conversion is to have a wash-hand basin in it, or to have a full bathroom, or to have radiators taken from the existing central heating system, then particular attention has to be paid to the plumbing works.

An existing roof space normally contains a single water tank to service the house and, possibly, a small expansion tank if there is central heating.

If a bathroom is to be installed then the main water tank must be raised higher than the bathroom units it is to service if a normal gravity feed system is to be used.

If radiators are to be incorporated into the conversion, then the expansion tank must also be raised higher than the radiators it is servicing. This means either that the water tanks must form part of the rooms and be raised up to the ceiling height or, if there is sufficient room above the ceiling collars, then the water tanks can be placed in the apex of the roof. Obviously, the latter can only be achieved on the assumption that there is a really good ridge height.

Another alternative for the positioning of the water tanks is on the flat roof of the dormers themselves, but there are very often planning objections to this and this must be checked out first.

If the water tanks cannot go into the apex of the roof or on it, one of the most convenient places for the positioning of the tanks is over the new stairs. This is dead space and can often be the most convenient position.

Water tanks are often a considerable source of irritation and it is as well to ensure that a first-class plumber is involved at the design stage. What can often appear to be a fairly simple 'tank shift' can end up a complicated and costly part of the exercise. Many of the older houses have old steel barrel or lead pipes and the labour content involved is much higher than in dealing with modern copper pipes and capillary fittings.

Because in many loft conversions the lateral space available is at a premium, many people think in terms of a shower rather than a bath. While the idea is quite sound the plumbing complications are often not really foreseen. There are plenty of manufacturers now producing showers that incorporate a water heater in the unit itself and which can therefore be fed off a rising main; however, the performance of the show-

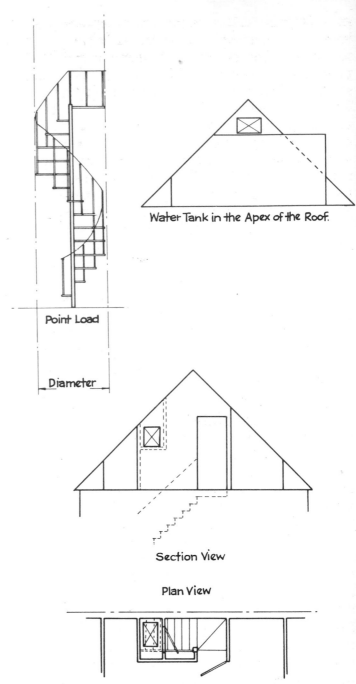

Water Tank in the Apex of the Roof.

Point Load

Diameter

Section View

Plan View

Water Tank positioned over New Stairwell.

er is often a lot less than desired. Most people's idea of a shower goes back to their school-days where after a good game of rugger one had a lovely hot shower. But a shower fed from water tanks in a roof down to the ground floor is a very different affair from a shower being fed from a water tank only a few feet above it. The rising main technique would seem to be an ideal solution, in that pressure from the mains water system gives a really good 'squirt'. The trouble is, though, that the water has to pass through a water heater and the more you turn it on and the faster the water comes through, the colder it gets. So that to have a really hot shower you end up getting just a dribble. Or, if you want to have a lot of water, then you must be prepared to be braced for a really good cold shower. The brochures always look terrific. There is some beautiful girl with lashings of steam all around her having a whale of a time. But, regrettably, you do not know how well the shower will work until the whole thing has been installed and you are about to use it. So do make sure that you get some sound advice from a really good plumber.

Basins can also be fed in the same way, but you will not be half as exasperated over a slow pressure for a basin as with a slow pressure from a shower. But a slow running bath will inevitably drive you mad. While baths, basins and showers may have their technical problems, the most difficult question to solve is the positioning of the lavatory. Waste water can be disposed of fairly easily, but soil from a lavatory is a very different matter.

A lavatory must obviously be connected to a soil vent pipe to dispose of the waste matter. Naturally enough one wants to connect to an existing soil vent pipe (S.V.P.) rather than running a new one and having to connect up at ground level with additional manholes. Therefore the positioning of a lavatory must of necessity be close to the existing S.V.P.

So far as the sanitary ware is concerned, there are many different shapes, styles and colours available on the market for the different units concerned. The same goes for all the fittings, and it is possible to browse through catalogues and get oneself beautifully confused before making a choice. It is ten-to-one on that your choice will end up being the one model that is not available, has been discontinued or is on a twenty-four week delivery. So by all means choose what you want but do be sure that delivery can be effected without holding up the building works.

ELECTRICS

The electrician plays a very straightforward role and generally there is very little that can go wrong. He normally turns up first when the crew is in the process of carcassing out the conversion, as that is the time when he wishes to lay all his cables. He then returns to pull all his wires through and

makes a final visit to connect all his switches, power points and fittings.

The electrical cost within the price of the conversion as a whole is very small and it is therefore better to err on the generous side than to try to save by not having exactly what you want.

At the design stage it is often difficult to visualise the number of power points you will need in a particular room. While an allowance of, say, two power points per room should be quite adequate it is much better to have more rather than not enough. Again, if an electrician is fitting a power point it is a very small marginal cost for him to fit a double power point at the same time. So, if anything, tend to have a good scattering of power points and if you think you would prefer to have wall lights rather than a pendant light from the ceiling, it is at the design stage that you should decide.

It is often easy to forget when considering a bathroom that you will need to have a strip light over the basin. At the same time, if you are going to have a strip light then you might as well have a strip light that incorporates an electric shaver. Always remember that it is very little additional cost to have exactly what you want at the time the electrician is on site and running his wires. But it is a very different picture to have to bring him back at a later date to ask him to provide some additional feature.

FINISH

The conversion should have a normal plastered finish. This means that any brickwork – for example, party walls – should be rendered and set and the plasterboard should be properly scrim jointed and skim coated. A very much cheaper finish is to have what is known as a dry-lined finish.

A dry-lined finish is definitely a second rate method which, although it is cheaper, certainly shows its economy. This method is possible where plasterboard has been used and the joints are merely filled with a standard filler which is then rubbed down so that you can then put lining paper on and paint or else put wallpaper straight on to it. The main problem is that however well you fill the joints they will always – and it must be repeated, always – be seen.

As long as you accept that this doesn't

matter, then a dry-line finish will certainly save bringing in a plasterer and might save you a couple of hundred pounds on the bill. If you are doing just a simple playroom for the children then it may be quite reasonable to finish the job in this way, but if you are having a bedroom and bathroom then there is no doubt that your conversion will deserve nothing less than a proper, plastered, finish.

With loft conversions there are always awkward angles around the dormers and along the sloping walls. So however good the carpenters may be, when it comes to tacking on the plasterboard they will always find it difficult to get a perfect joint. Therefore, it can be seen that by simply filling the joint one is not eradicating the problem. However, a really good plasterer will be able to feather over the unevenness and so ensure a high quality finish. Mind you, if he is a lousy plasterer you may well wish you had saved your money and had a dry-lined finish!

The whole thing about plastering is that it is a messy business. There is no doubt that with plaster slopping around all over the place it is difficult to keep the floor clean. It is especially difficult to stop the plaster running down the walls when the new work over the staircase meets the old work. It is quite inevitable that you will be involved in a certain amount of re-decoration but then it

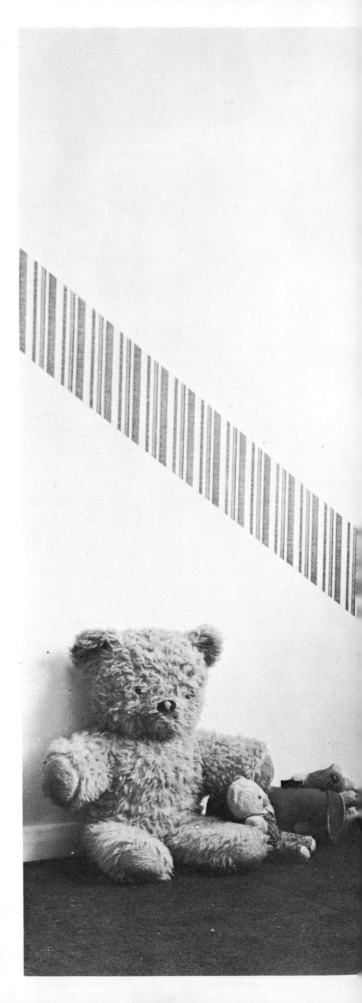

Striped wallpaper accentuates the angles in dormer rooms.

is doubtful that a dry-line finish would save you that, anyway. So when the plasterer turns up with his hop-up and his hawk to commence battle, make sure that there are plenty of dust sheets!

Other aspects to be considered at the time of the finish of the construction work are things like skirting boards, architraves and door furniture. With the price that prepared timber is now, there is a great tendency to cheat over skirting and architrave work. Very often only basic skirting is given rather than carefully matching in with the rest of the house and the architraves around the doors are often very mean and uninteresting. Door furniture is very much a matter of taste. It is very usual nowadays to have lever latch handles, but so often proper brass knobs look very much better.

PAINTING AND DECORATING

The wallpaper and painting form the final finish. Nowadays, as everyone appears to be the original 'do-it-yourselfer', this is at least an area where you can genuinely save money in terms of labour. In a majority of cases the only difference between the professional decorator and the D.I.Y. home decorator is the length of time it takes for the job to be done.

However, if you are having the decoration done professionally, then do make sure that all the building works are rubbed down properly and all the joints and stops are filled before any decorating has been started. It is definitely true to say that the best decorating jobs are the ones that have been properly prepared first.

It is perfectly reasonable for you to decorate on the inside, but when it comes to the external fascia boards around the dormer, and possibly even the external parts of the windows, it is far better to ensure that this is done when scaffolding and ladders are on site for the actual construction work. So, whoever is doing your conversion, do make sure that even if the painting and decorating is not to be done on the inside, they do at least do the outside for you.

The angles that dormer windows produce make for interesting potential in terms of decorating. However, taste is a very personal matter and the size of one's bank balance has an awful lot to do with it! Striped

Below: This penthouse conversion produced a delightful master bedroom which was well lit by two sets of french windows opening onto a balcony. The furniture and fittings as much as the decor make the final effect most attractive.

wallpaper can produce a most interesting effect (see photographs on pages 30/31).

Patterned wallpaper with coving around the ceiling often brings out the best for bedrooms (see photo on previous page).

Where a hollow joisted ceiling has been incorporated into the room, the beams can have a striking effect if either painted in contrast to the ceiling or else sanded down and polyurethaned.

The two previous chapters have been summarised at the end to help the reader. With this chapter the best summary is perhaps in the form of case histories of examples of the different forms of conversions that follow in the next chapter.

Chapter IV

Case histories

Case History No. I

Basic Type
Detached gable-to-gable.

Features
Large 30 ft (9·1 m) dormer with staircase rising from a first floor room.

Building Control
Building Regulations.

The reason for the conversion was to provide a master bedroom and bathroom for the owners of the property. The preliminary survey showed a tremendous potential since the property was a gable-to-gable construction. The overall length of the house was 36 ft (11·0 m) and at the plane of 3 ft 6 ins (1·07 m) a width of 15 ft (4·5 m) could be achieved. It was indeed fortunate that there were three load bearing walls breaking the span of the trusses. The ridge height was quite adequate, but because of the length of the ridge it was necessary to incorporate a flitched beam in the apex of the roof.

Because the existing stairwell was approximately in the centre and to the front of the house, it meant that any staircase rising over it would automatically break the conversion above into two. At the same time it would mean a much larger dormer to the front in order to bring the staircase up. It was decided that the stairs would rise from an existing bedroom on the first floor so that they should arrive at one of the gable ends. As you will see from the drawing this meant that a large bedroom with a through bathroom could be produced, giving the optimum usable floor space.

There is no doubt that the addition of the large dormer enhanced the external appearance of the house, because the original roof was very plain and ordinary and the dormer

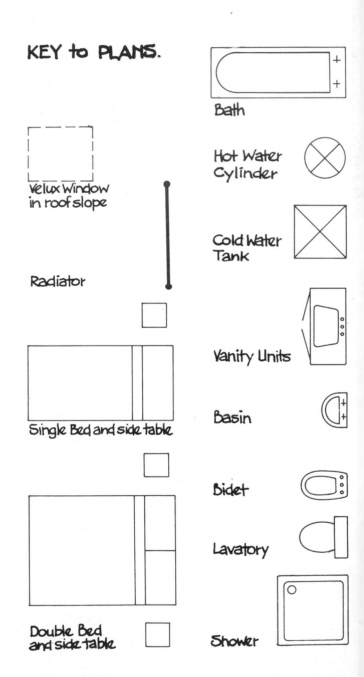

KEY to PLANS.

Velux Window in roof slope

Radiator

Single Bed and side table

Double Bed and side table

Bath

Hot Water Cylinder

Cold Water Tank

Vanity Units

Basin

Bidet

Lavatory

Shower

gave character to the building as a whole. The further addition of leaded lights set off the whole conversion.

The dormer has blended in extremely well with the conversion and this is a good example of using tiles hung vertically in

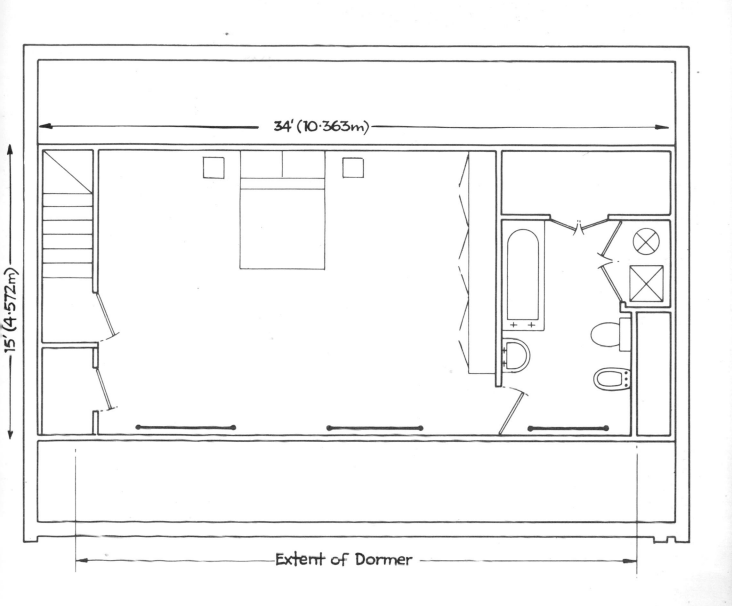

34' (10·363m)

15' (4·572m)

Extent of Dormer

Left: Because the existing roof was covered with pantiles, they could not be vertically hung on the dormer.

between the windows and on the cheeks of the dormer. You will appreciate immediately how much less room could have been achieved had this house been a hip-to-hip structure, even though the floor space would have been the same.

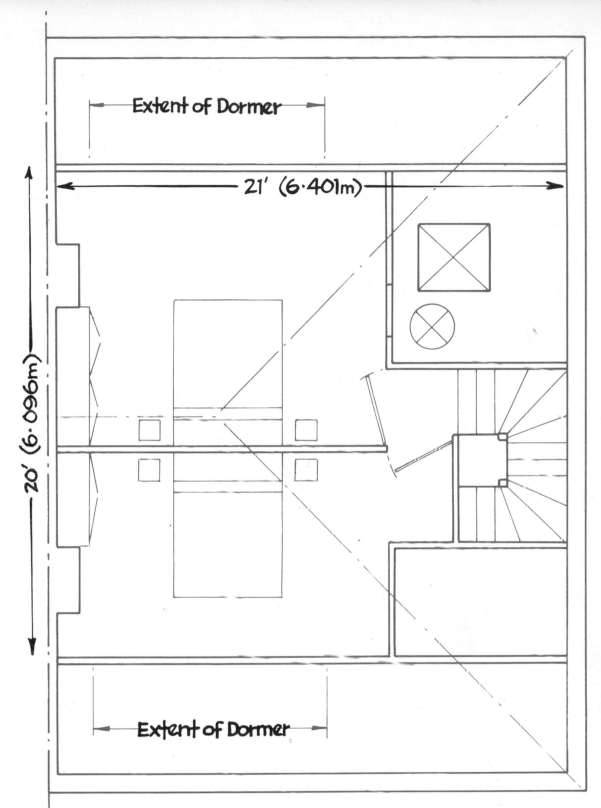

Extent of Dormer

21' (6·401m)

20' (6·096m)

Extent of Dormer

Case History No. II

Basic Type
Semi-detached hip-to-gable.

Features
*Through dormers, front and rear with bay
dormer on the hip for stair access.*

Building Control
Building Regulations.

This conversion was designed to produce
two additional bedrooms with the new stairs
following over the stairs which rose on the
outside flank walls. A good ridge height of
10 ft 6 ins (3·2 m) and a central load bearing
wall ensured that the conversion was feasible. While the front and rear dormers are
quite attractive and blend in with the house,
this is not true of the large bay dormer on
the hip of the house, which is only there to

produce the necessary stair access from the landing below. However, because the three dormers are all tiled in with matching tiles, it at least minimises the 'stuck-on' effect.

Trussed purlins were used and because the span was less than 23 ft (7·0 m) no load bearing wall was required. However, the span between the trusses amounted to 20 ft (6·1 m) and it was fortunate that the central load bearing wall was there so that the size of joist could be cut to no more than 7 ins × 2 ins (177 mm × 50 mm) except for the trimmers where 10 ins × 3 ins (254 mm × 76 mm) joists were required. (On a similar conversion carried out in the same locality, the house did not have the central load bearing wall and joists of a tremendous size – 11 ins × 3 ins (279 mm × 76 mm) were required. Not only were they extremely heavy and difficult to position but, of course, costs went up considerably. Although to all intents and purposes the end result was exactly the same as this conversion it in fact cost quite a bit more because of the difference in structure.)

The staircase followed neatly over the existing stairs and required two sets of winders in order to turn back on itself so that a landing could be formed for access to the two rooms. The staircase was naturally designed to follow the similar lines of the existing one so that the internal appearance would make any visitor think that the house was an original three-storey building.

Because no wash hand basin or central heating was required in the new conversion, it was possible to site the water tanks in the eves of the roof under the hip.

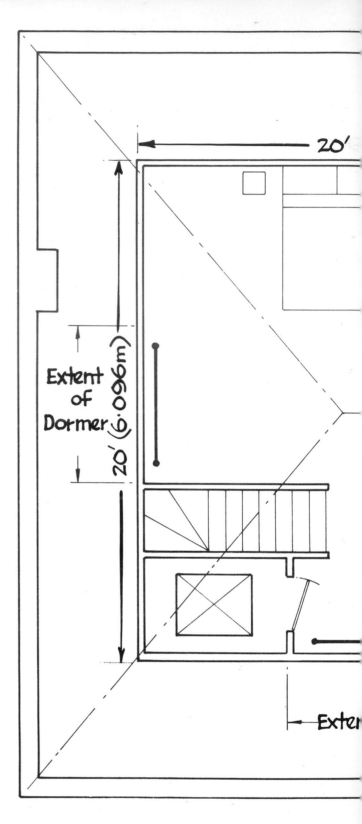

Left: This is a good example of dormers draining back onto the main roof, instead of into the gutters on the front facia. Note the contrast of the corner tiles (see also page 18).

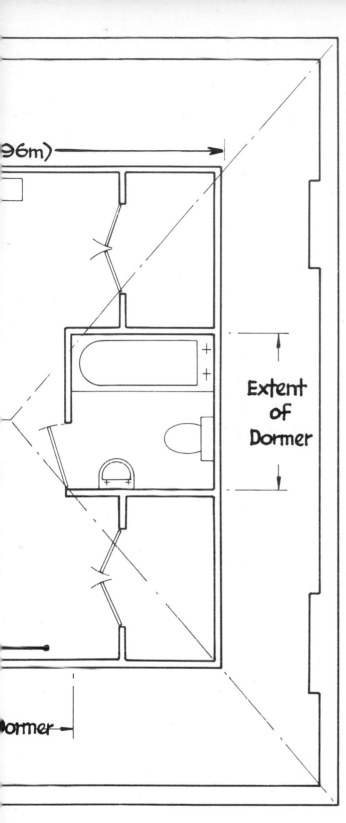

96m) →

Extent
of
Dormer

ormer —

Case History No. III

Basic Type
Hip-to-hip.

Features
Three dormer windows, staircase within room.

Building Control
Inner London.

The house was situated at the end of a row of houses and the views from the south and west sides of the building were particularly attractive since they looked over a park. The first reaction was to design the staircase so that it followed over the existing stairs – but this meant that the dormer on the west side would be used purely for the staircase and would be of no benefit for the actual room. It was decided that the stairs would rise parallel to the existing staircase by dismantling an airing cupboard and foreshortening the bathroom on the first floor. The existing bathroom and separate w.c. were made into one and the airing cupboard foreshortened to allow the stairs to rise up into the conversion. In this way the dormer to the west side of the property formed part of the bedroom as, of course, did the dormer to the south. The dormer on the east side, which overlooked the adjoining property, was where the new bathroom was positioned.

Because of the way the staircase rose into the room it was decided that the door would be at the foot of the stairs and the staircase would rise in such a way that it did not properly dissect the room as it might otherwise have done. The well of the stairs was balustraded and, in fact, added an interesting dimension to the room as a whole.

The conversion utilised four trusses and gave a total floor area of 20 ft × 20 ft (6·1 m × 6·1 m). Fortunately, the house had a good proportion of load bearing walls which broke the spans of the walls, giving good stability to this quite large loft conversion. Because the ridge height was just over 12 ft (3·7 m), it was possible to design a ceiling joist plan of sufficient strength to take the water tanks under the apex of the roof. Thus, the bathroom could be fed properly and the central heating brought up into the new third floor.

The bed was positioned under the sloping roof to the front so that the full benefit of the

41

views to the south and west of the property could be realised. The owners considered the conversion a great success in that it not only gave them exactly what they wanted internally, but it also added a great deal of character to the house externally. Because the roof was of considerable size there is no doubt that the dormers blended in very well and since the existing tiles were re-used on the cheeks of the dormers, the general appearance was as if the house had been built in that way originally.

Case History No. IV

Basic Type
End-of-terrace and gable-to-gable.

Features
Brick bay dormer to the rear of the property. Staircase following over existing staircase.

Building Control
Inner London.

This end-of-terrace property could only just be converted within the ridge of the roof as permitted development. Because of its location planning permission would have taken a considerable time and there would have been a serious doubt that consent would have been given as it would have been the first conversion of its sort in the street. However, the ridge height just allowed the conversion to take place and the size was such that a bedroom and bathroom could be produced, providing a large brick built bay dormer was incorporated to the rear.

The two parapet walls to the sides of the property had to be built up. So did the rear wall to allow a dormer to be constructed from the ridge. This made full use of the space available and allowed the staircase to rise over the existing one to give entry at one corner. A small dormer was designed to the front of the property to give further headroom and through light to the conversion. No load bearing walls were available so two steel beams had to be used to break the spans. Because the property was an end-of-terrace it was very simple for a crane to slide both steels through the end of the flank wall to be

Above: The alcove to the left of the picture was originally to have been a storage cupboard but instead was incorporated into the room as an intriguing dimension.

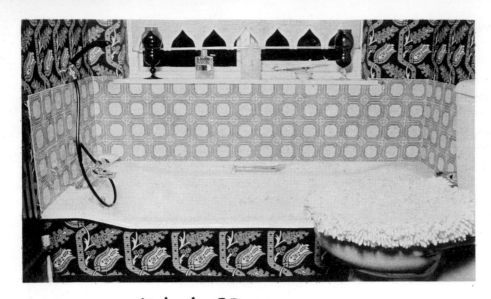

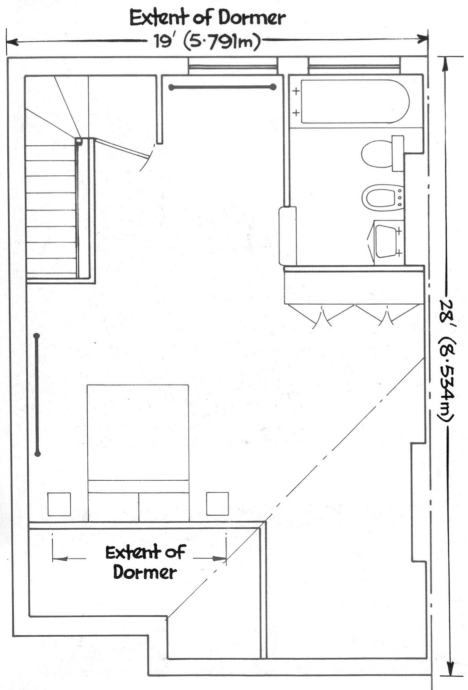

Extent of Dormer

19' (5.791m)

28' (8.534m)

Extent of
Dormer

positioned within the party wall of the adjoining property.

The client wanted to have a sunken bath and this was achieved by raising the whole of the bathroom floor by one foot (30 cms) and sinking the bath on to the joists of the main conversion. An archway entrance into the bathroom gave a particularly pleasant effect.

The whole ceiling was designed with the ceiling collars made of prepared timber so that they could be exposed and picked out as a feature. This concept is known as a 'hollow joisted ceiling' and it is particularly useful where there is a minimum of room with regard to the ridge height of the building.

It is a more costly exercise but a definite effect is created which with good interior design and decoration, can be very attractive. The staircase was designed with particular care and the existing balusters matched to blend in with the house.

The front dormer was faced with shiplap boarding and painted white to contrast with the grey slates. As it was an end-of-terrace house the dormer would be more pronounced and it was considered much better that this should be accentuated, rather than to try to hide the dormer by facing it with slate.

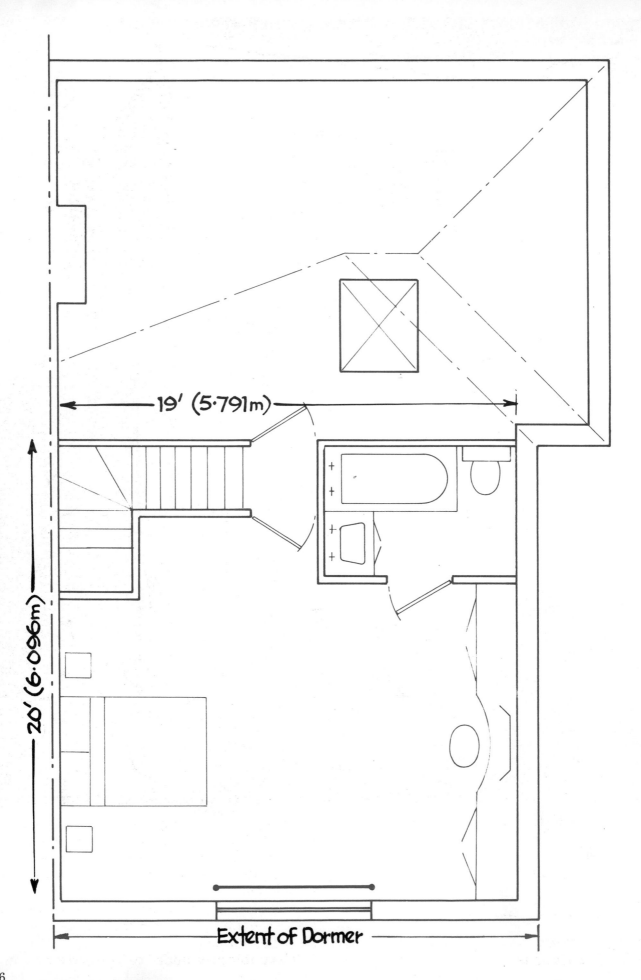

19' (5·791m)

20' (6·096m)

Extent of Dormer

Case History No. V

Basic Type
Semi-detached hip-to-gable.

Features
Large brick built bay dormer.

Building Control
Building Regulations.

This is a good example of a brick built bay dormer blending in very well with the property, despite its size in comparison with the original roof. This is mainly because there is brickwork on two elevations rather than as in Case History No. II where the bay dormer coming out from the roof is therefore very pronounced.

The cubic area added to the house was only

47

just within the permitted development ruling and it shows how much can be added to the house without planning consent being required. The overall conversion was nearly 20 ft (6·1 m) square and it is interesting to note that the whole of it was at the full 7 ft 7 ins (2·3 m) floor-to-ceiling height. At the same time a considerable storage area was produced and it was possible to site the tanks within this area at a height that would allow the bathroom to be fed.

The staircase followed over the existing stairs at the cost of losing a small cupboard on the first floor landing. Once again, the staircase was carefully matched and blended in very well with the property as a whole. This is an example where winders and a quarter landing were used and the same newel posts picked up.

The new bedroom turned out to be the largest room in the house but unfortunately there were no load bearing walls to break the span of joists. Without using steel work, this meant that the joist sizes had to be 11 ins × 3 ins (279 mm × 76 mm) – a sturdy structure, indeed! While the front and sides of the dormer were rendered and set with pebble dash and painted white, the cheek to the rear was tiled so that it blended in with the rear roof as viewed from the garden. Incidentally, it was only cost that prevented the rear roof from being stripped and a sizeable patio garden produced.

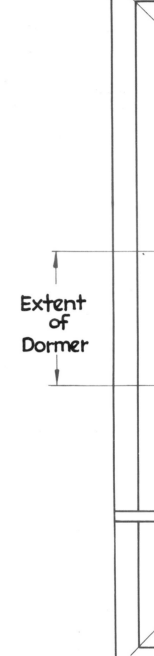

Extent of Dormer

Case History No. VI

Basic Type
Detached house hip-to-hip.

Features
Two through dormers with a hipped dormer for bathroom.

Building Control
Building Regulations.

Although a hipped property, quite a considerable usable floor area was achieved on a four trussed construction utilising load bearing walls to break the span. The staircase rose over the existing stairs and, by the use of one set of winders and a quarter landing, arrived in such a position as to allow access to a good sized bedroom and a small bathroom situated within the hip.

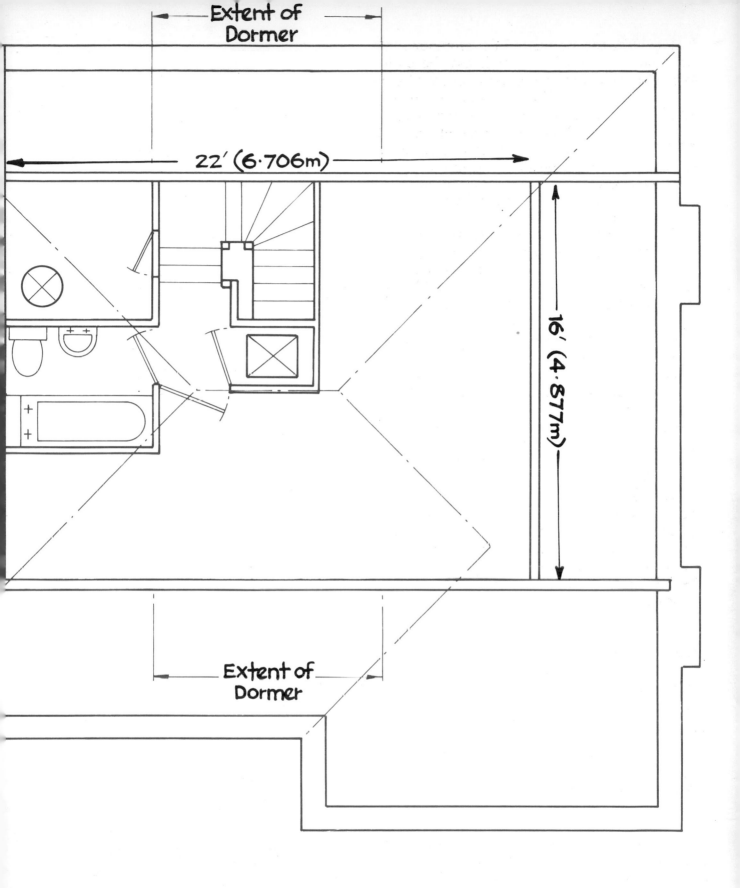

Extent of
Dormer

22' (6·706m)

16' (4·877m)

Extent of
Dormer

*Left: This house has a third dormer to the rear (as can be
seen on the plan above) and it takes a good ridge height to
get the essential stability.*

The bedroom formed an 'L' shape and utilised not only the large dormer to the front but also part of the dormer over the staircase to the rear (an exactly similar conversion on the house next door also incorporated a Velux window in the hip in the bedroom for further light and ventilation).

Because sufficient head room could not be found within the apex of the roof for the water tanks, a cupboard had to be built off the landing to raise up the tanks so that the bathroom could be fed. This used up valuable space in the main body of the conversion. If the ridge height had been just that much higher it would have been possible (as in Case History No. III) to have placed the water tanks within the apex and thus to have increased the space available.

Again, it was possible to make the dormers blend in very closely with the house by incorporating leaded light windows as on the floor below – also by ensuring that the cheeks of the dormers were tiled.

Case History No. VII

Basic Type
End-of-terrace gable-to-gable

Features
Bay dormer with sliding windows on to balcony

Building Control
Building Regulations.

Without in any way spoiling the front elevation, which has a bonnet protruding over a bay window, the roof space was fully used by producing a bay dormer to the rear of the property and cantilevering a balcony on to it. The bay dormer was set in from the two sides and was faced with shiplap boarding painted white so that it would contrast with the overall grey appearance of the terrace as a whole.

The stairs rose over the existing stairs but it was necessary to re-position the two doors into the two main bedrooms on the first floor to achieve proper access. Using a set of winders at the top of the stairs a small landing was created for access into the bedroom. After the conversion was built the owner went

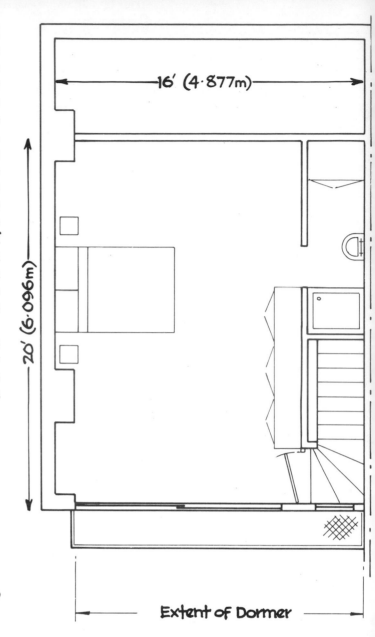

Above: The interior of the penthouse

Left: Although this is an imposing dormer, the large aluminium sliding windows made a light and airy room.

on to add a small shower unit behind the stairs and so was able to turn the conversion into 'her own pad'.

The sliding windows let a lot of light into the room and being able to step out on to the small balcony is an added pleasure.

Case History No. VIII

Basic Type
Mid-terrace, centre valley.

Features
Penthouse with balcony.

Building Control
Inner London.

It took just over a year to get planning consent for this conversion and while the

end result really is extremely good, the fight to get permission to do it was quite appalling. The immediate advantage of a penthouse is that the whole conversion is at the full headroom – there are no hips or valleys to contend with.

The staircase followed over the existing stairs by using a half landing and it was originally intended that the bathroom should be built up over the existing rear extension of the house. However, planning would not allow this and so space had to be found within the penthouse itself.

The water tanks were positioned on the roof so it was easy to feed the bathroom and the central heating which was taken up off the existing system. The conversion had to be set back from the front of the road – hence the balcony with parapet – and it also had to be set back from the rear because Planning would not allow the centre valley shape of the building to disappear. While one can accept the very sensible reasons for the angle of the parapet to the front of the property, it

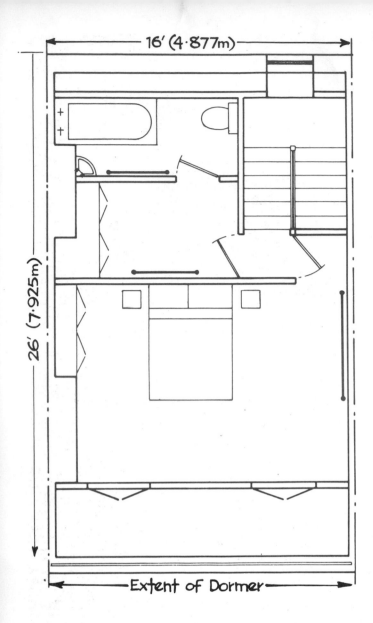

16' (4·877m)

26' (7·925m)

← Extent of Dormer →

Above: Plan of penthouse master bedroom, dressing room and bathroom suite.

still remains a mystery as to why there was so much fuss over the rear elevations.

The bedroom itself turned out to be an exceptionally pleasant room and the two sets of french windows opening onto the balcony were most effective. The old Victorian staircase was carefully copied and this attention to detail paid off.

It is interesting to see these Victorian terraces in the centre of London being developed in this way, because there would otherwise be every likelihood that they would fall into a developer's hands and be bulldozed to the ground to make way for new development schemes.

Case History No. IX

Basic Type
Detached hip-to-hip with central flat roof.

Features
Large natural headroom under flat roof.

Building Control
Inner London.

As the photograph above shows this is a very large detached house with a considerable loft area. The dormer windows were hardly necessary to achieve the headroom but they blended in well with the house and gave much more character than the Velux windows did on the other side of the house.

The staircase rose from the floor below to a small landing, giving access to two bedrooms with a bathroom en suite with the main bedroom.

The main bedroom did not require a dormer at all and was very well lit by two Velux windows. The bathroom needed a dormer for headroom and so the smaller bedroom also had a dormer to provide a proper balance when viewed from outside. The house had a considerable number of load bearing walls and, indeed, the two large chimneys were load bearing, so that no trusses or large steel beams were required. At both ends of the conversion considerable storage areas were produced and the converted area amounted to more than 500 sq. ft (47 sq. m).

This is a fine example of dead space being put into commission and although two sizeable bedrooms and a bathroom were added to the house, no planning consent was required because the addition of the two small dormers was, of course, well within the permitted development rule.

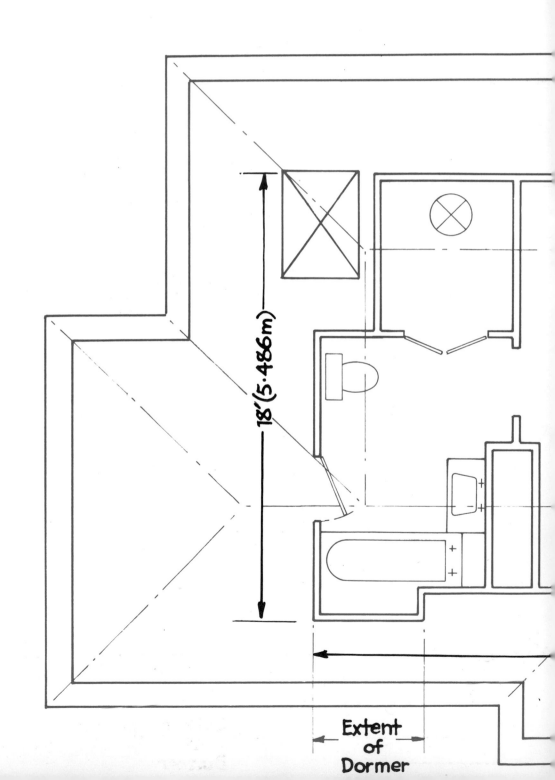

18' (5.486m)

Extent of Dormer

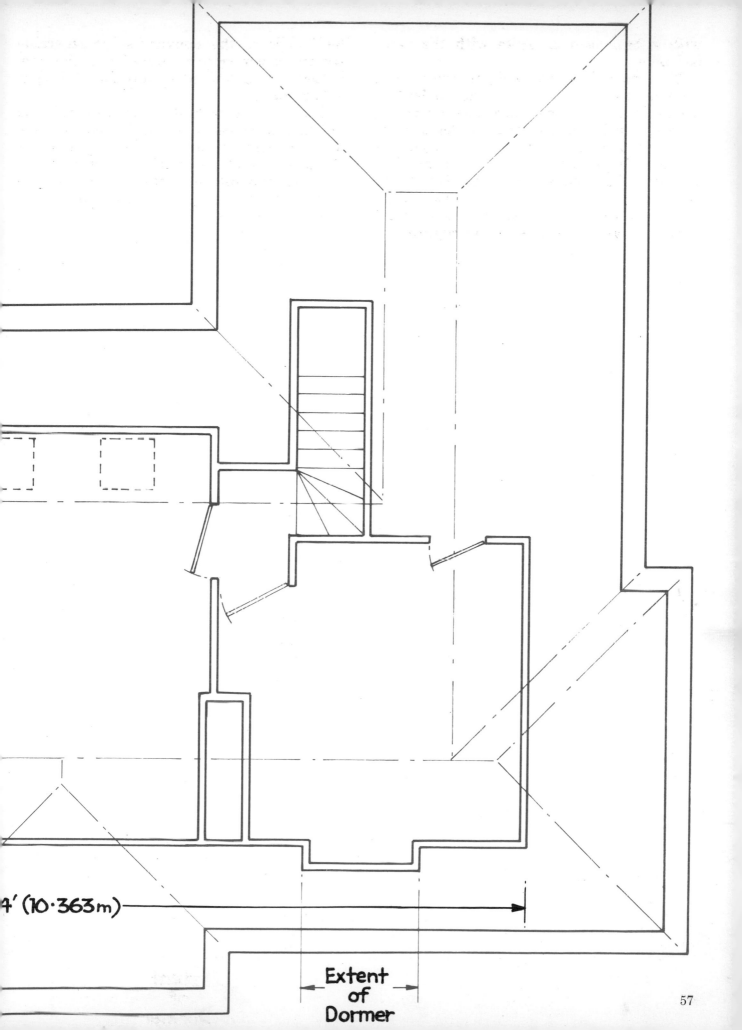

4' (10·363m)

Extent
of
Dormer

Case History No. X

Basic Type
Detached hip-to-hip

Features
Dismantling existing roof and totally redesigning with a Mansard type construction.

Building Control
Inner London.

This was a difficult and costly conversion, but it achieved a considerable addition to the property without altering the front elevation. You will see from the dotted lines of the sectional plan below that the original ridge height was just too low to achieve the mandatory headroom. You will also notice that the headroom and the large chimney further reduced the potential of the existing structure.

The obvious thing to do was to dismantle the whole of the existing structure from the front roof slope. This meant that the ridge could be raised and a Mansard type roof constructed, thereby allowing a large conversion to be achieved. The end result from the rear elevation is as the photograph overleaf. The windows blended in very well with the house even if the overall character had considerably changed from what it was.

More than seven hundred square feet (65 sq. m) of additional accommodation were provided by way of three bedrooms, a bathroom and a playroom. The staircase rose over the existing stairs and, to avoid taking away the next door neighbour's light, an angled shaft equivalent to the old roof slope had to be produced instead of a dormer. As the floor plan shows, even the front roof slope yielded a useful storage area.

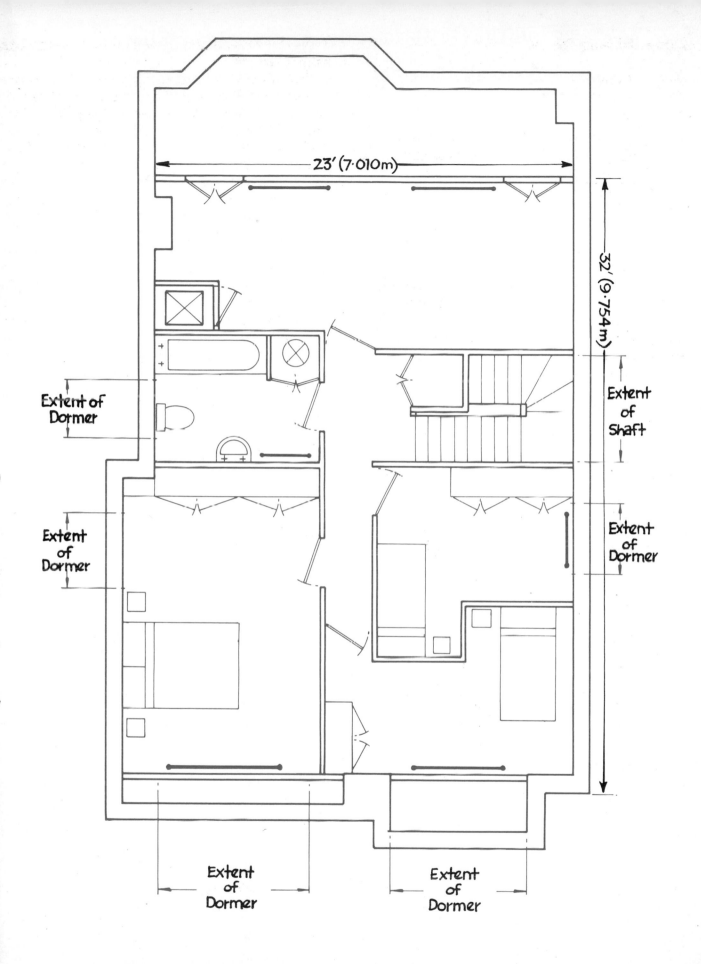

23' (7·010m)

32' (9·754m)

Extent of Dormer

Extent of Dormer

Extent of Shaft

Extent of Dormer

Extent of Dormer

Extent of Dormer

Left: A large conversion that added a whole floor to the house (see previous page).

Above: A typical conversion which can be seen in thousands of terraces in the big cities.

Case History No. XI

Basic Type
End-of-terrace gable-to-gable.

Features
Centralized single dormer with slate hung cheeks and shiplap facing.

Building Control
Building Regulations.

This is a very common type of conversion within the big cities and although an obvious addition to the property, the dormer sits well within the roof slope. It would be worth comparing this conversion with the one achieved in Case History No. VII. As you can see, a much larger conversion can be produced – but with a much more dramatic effect on the exterior elevation.

The staircase rose over the existing stairs and the pitch of the roof was such that no dormer was required for headroom. This

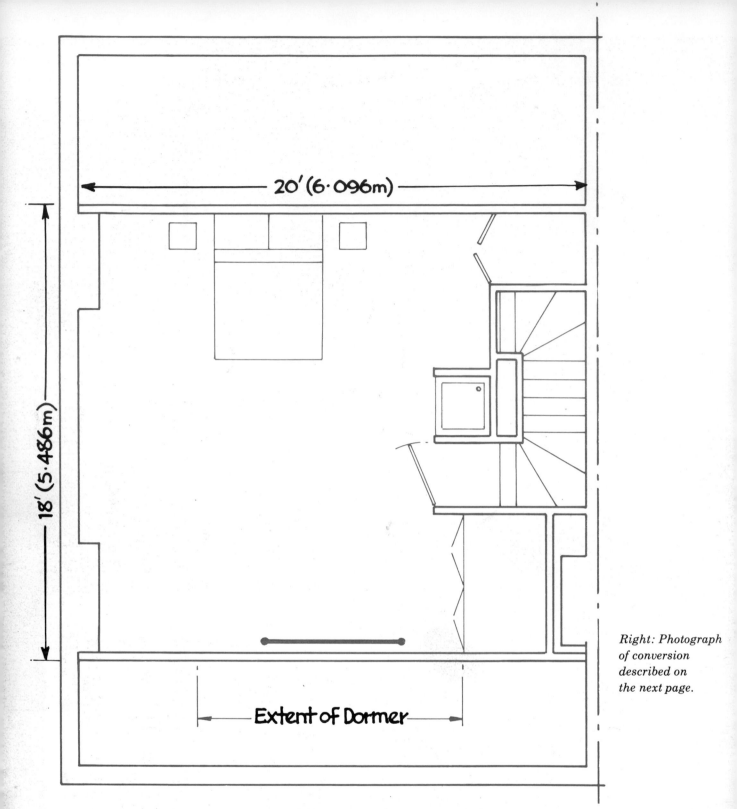

20' (6·096m)

18' (5·486m)

Extent of Dormer

Right: Photograph of conversion described on the next page.

meant that the size and positioning of the dormer were purely matters of choice rather than of necessity. The front roof slope was not touched and, as you will see from the plan above, the shower was fitted by the entrance to the room rather than behind the stairs because of the headroom. It might have been better to have had the shower in that position – but this would have necessitated a dormer to the front.

The overall size of the conversion was 18 ft × 20 ft (5·5 m × 6·1 m) with an 11 ft (3·5 m) dormer. This conversion must be a prime example of how a very ordinary house can achieve an additional bedroom without encroaching on the small amount of garden to the rear of the property. It makes one wonder whether, if more of this work were done, we would have the housing shortage that we have at the moment in this country.

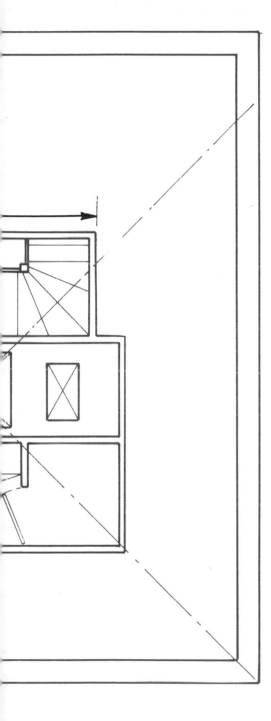

Case History No. XII

Basic Type
Detached hip-to-hip.

Features
Two through dormers the entire width of the ridge: one bay and one standard.

Building Control
Inner London.

The large bay dormer to the rear of the property is, in reality, not half as imposing as the photograph shows. The front dormer fitted neatly into the roof slope but the bay dormer was essential if the amount of space desired was to be achieved.

The existing staircase and landing was to the front of the house and it was not possible to design the new staircase to arrive over the existing one without having a bay dormer to the front. Therefore a lavatory on the first floor was re-positioned and the space created allowed the staircase to rise up in the position shown on the plan left. This allowed the two bedrooms and bathroom to come off the landing, as well as giving access to the water tanks positioned by the side of the staircase. A small box room with a Velux window fitted into the hip of the roof was also created.

The heavy pantiled roof and the large spans that were involved meant that a combination of trussed purlins and steel work was required to achieve the essential structural stability. The dormers were 17 ft (5·2 m) wide and the ridge height only just sufficient for the collars to come underneath it. However, once the basic structure was sorted out and the district surveyor was satisfied with the loadings, a very worthwhile addition to the property was achieved. The client spent much time and energy ensuring that the finished interior decoration was to an exceptional standard, as the photograph of the bathroom shows. A well known firm of decorators were brought in and made an outstanding job of it.

The photograph on page 24 was part of this conversion as well as the photograph on page 30. My dear father used to say 'it is just a matter of money' but, quite honestly,

it's a little bit more than that in the sense that it depends on one's taste and the skill of the men doing the job.

Case History No. XIII

Basic Type
Detached hip-to-hip.

Features
Thirty-four foot (ten metre) dormer with balcony running the full length.

Building Control
Building Regulations.

The story behind this conversion has an interesting bearing on the final design. This was a case of a widow with a family marrying a widower with a family and, pretty obviously, requiring more living accommodation. When they first considered the idea of a loft conversion it was to put the children upstairs in the new conversion. However, after discussing the pros and cons, they decided on a new master bedroom, dressing room and bathroom complex for themselves – rearranging the existing first floor to take the expanding family.

The existing first floor landing ran the length of the house to the front and it was not possible to consider putting the staircase up over the existing stairs. Instead, one of the bedrooms on the first floor was foreshortened by 3 ft (91·4 cm) so that the staircase could rise off the landing and turn in such a way that it dissected the floor area of the loft. Thus, a small landing was created with access on either side.

A very well-proportioned bedroom was produced and the sliding doors onto a balcony were obviously a particular feature – especially as the balcony overlooked a spacious lawn and woods. The roof sloping to the front of the house was filled with fitted cupboards so that the general appearance of the bedroom was like an ordinary standard room at full height all round. For the finished

Left: This unusual bathroom with dazzling decor was part of the conversion on the previous page.

Above: The dressing room had its own wash basin and built-in units. There was also a door through to the lavatory.

Left: An imposing conversion that added a complete master bedroom suite that overlooked the spacious lawns and grounds of this country house.

This is a long and lean conversion which was neatly
divided by the staircase rising from the landing below. A
large, well-proportioned master bedroom was achieved,
plus a bathroom, dressing room and separate lavatory.
The plan belongs to Case History No. XIII.

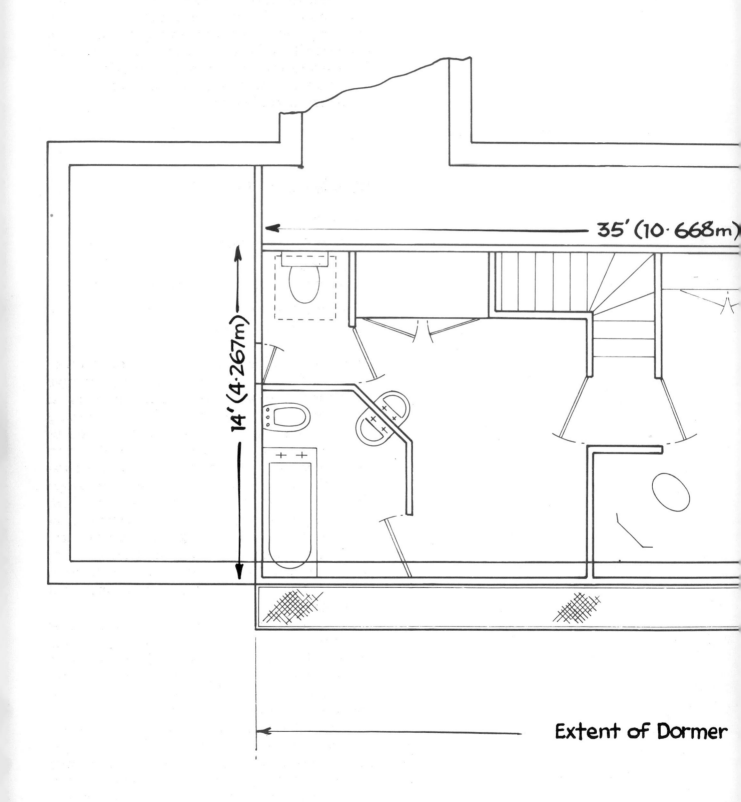

35' (10·668m)

14' (4·267m)

Extent of Dormer

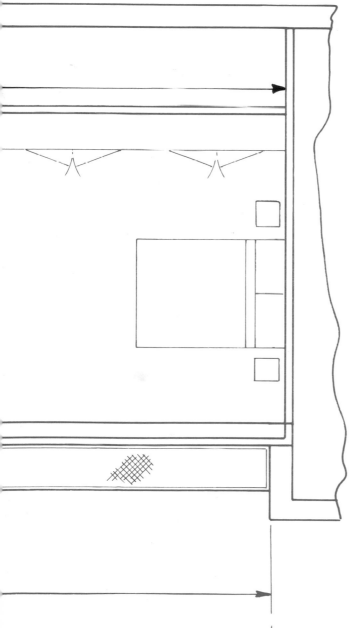

effect see the photograph on page 33 and front cover. The reason the new third storey was not made totally en suite was because of the size of the family and the potential value of having access to the bathroom without disturbing the master bedroom. Any man will appreciate the luxury of a dressing room and the ability to shave in peace while milady steams up the bathroom! A separate lavatory was also provided with a Velux window giving light and ventilation in the front roof slope.

Case History No. XIV

Basic Type
Bungalow hip-to-hip.

Features
Ridge extension to form a crowned dormer.

Building Control
Building Regulations.

The before and after photographs show quite clearly what was done externally, but give little idea as to the extent of the conversion internally. The removal of the existing chimney and the extension of the ridge to produce a crowned dormer produced a very neat conversion. The original thought was to go further and dismantle the lower roof slope over the extended part of the house and form a complete patio garden, but a covenant on the house allowed the next door neighbours to make a formal objection. Incidentally, the local authority could not have objected, since the total scheme came within permitted development.

Putting in a staircase in a bungalow usually means that some room or other has to be affected. However, with no existing staircase to have to match, it does mean that the style and type of staircase selected is completely optional. The staircase can be a modern open plan staircase and will in no way be affected by the fire regulations – as in the case of a house going from two storeys to three. In this particular case a close tread staircase rising from the hall was chosen but, in fact, it might equally have been an open plan staircase rising out of one of the rooms. As with most bungalows, all the walls were

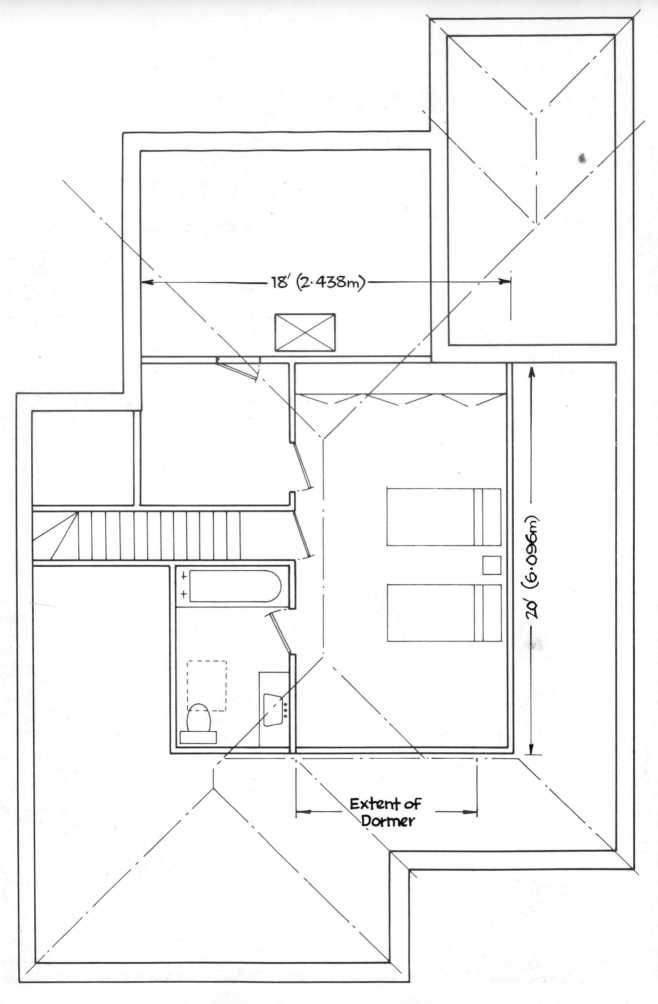

18' (2·438m)

20' (6·096m)

Extent of
Dormer

These photographs were taken by the client himself before the work started in the winter and on conclusion in the summer. They were taken from the same position. Observe how neatly this crowned dormer fitted in and, as the plan shows, what a very worthwhile conversion it gave.

load bearing and therefore the spans involved in creating the loft conversion were much reduced.

The overall measurement of the conversion was 18 ft × 20 ft (5·5 m × 6·1 m) and the bedroom and bathroom provided could be turned into a self-contained unit if the small box room, also incorporated, were to be turned into a small kitchenette. This sort of conversion is ideal for self-containing the mother-in-law problem if it falls to your lot to have to deal with it. In these inflationary times it can also house the grant-aided student or help you to rake in a few shekels by turning it into a *pied à terre* for some Common Market super salesman from Düsseldorf.

* * *

In these case histories I have tried to demonstrate what can be achieved across a very wide range of houses and buildings. Lofts, as we have seen, come in all sizes and shapes and most spare space can, with an agile imagination, good luck on the part of your planning application and ingenious building techniques, be put to good use.

You may, of course, find yourself in that unlucky minority group who simply can't contrive, without really awkward costs, the attic room of their dreams. But in most cases it is possible to do something. All the cases quoted have undoubtedly added considerably to the value of the respective properties. All the families concerned have found more room for living.

There is something truly adventurous about putting in a loft room. Perhaps we are all at heart secret architects. Perhaps making an extra room of our own imagining appeals to the eternal child in us. Yes – it can be difficult. But it's fun!

Chapter V
Building control

Until 1965 when the Building Regulations were introduced, all buildings came under local building byelaws and the rules varied from area to area. The Building Regulations came into force as a section of the Public Health Act introduced by the Government in 1961 but excluded the twelve London Boroughs forming the Greater London Council, as follows: Camden, Greenwich, Hackney, Hammersmith, Islington, Kensington and Chelsea, Lambeth, Lewisham, Southwark, Tower Hamlets, Wandsworth and the City of Westminster. It also excluded Scotland which has its own enabling Act (Building (Scotland) Act 1959) from which the Building Standards (Scotland) Regulations are derived. However, the substance of the Scottish regulations is similar to England and Wales.

The Building Regulations are, therefore, national in character and cannot be altered by local authorities, although they do have the power to relax certain regulations without reference to the Ministry. The London Building Acts Constructional Byelaws are administered by district surveyors and although the regulations are older in concept they are just as up to date as the Building Regulations. They call for similar information from designers and builders and take note of British Standards and Codes of Practice.

The Building Regulations are there to ensure that buildings are designed and constructed in such a manner as to protect the health and safety of both occupants and the public at large. The implementation of the Building Regulations is under the control of the local council and is currently paid for out of rates and taxes.

Each local authority has a building control department and the supervision of building works is carried out by building control officers. In the Inner London area the district surveyors and their assistants are responsible for ensuring that the building works are carried out in accordance with the constructional byelaws. Their service is paid for by the builders (a percentage of their building costs) and such is the wording of many of the clauses that the interpretation of many of the byelaws is 'to the satisfaction of the District Surveyor' and thus his word, *de facto*, is law.

Therefore, through the Public Health Acts and the London Building Acts, the local authority is the guardian of the public wellbeing and must be satisfied that any proposed building work complies with the law. The Building Regulations are constantly under review and, in fact, the Health and Safety at Work etc., Act which received the Royal Assent on July 31, 1974, will have a particular significance for the future. Part III of the Act enables the scope, purposes and coverage of the Building Regulations to be increased and allows for the inclusion of a number of improvements to make the procedures of Building Control more flexible.

For example, there is a definite intention that the building control will not be paid for by the local council out of rates and taxes but will be paid by the builder as is at present done in the Inner London area. However, the bringing into force of the whole of Part III and the making and amendment of regulations under the new powers will be spread over some years and it is important to realise that the coming into force of any of the new provisions will depend upon the announcement of a commencement order. As yet no such order has been made and, therefore, the Building Regulations stand as they are with the Inner London area under the London Building Acts.

Generally, the British Standards state the requirements of materials, such as strength, size, shape and durability. The Codes of Practice fall under two main headings: those that recommend on the functional requirements of building, such as imposed load and wind load to be considered in the design of the structure, and those which recommend design criteria to be adopted in using a particular material. For instance, there are Codes of Practice for reinforced concrete, timber in building, load bearing brickwork and foundations. The use of materials to British Standards and the design to Codes of Practice are accepted as meeting the requirements of the Building Regulations.

Before you start any building works involving structural alterations it is mandatory that you deposit plans with the local authority. It is also necessary, under the Building Regulations, to give at least seven days notice in writing before building works commence. District surveyors only require two days notice – although it is wise to submit the plans well in advance so that any queries can be sorted out.

When plans are deposited under the Building Regulations, the local authority must pass the plans unless they are defective in that they do not comply with the Regulations or Public Health Acts or that they do not show that the proposed building works will in fact comply with them.

If the plans show that the proposed work will contravene any of the regulations then, of course, they will be rejected. The period within which the plans must be passed or rejected by the local authority is five weeks from the date of the deposit of the plans, but the local authority may ask for an extension of time to deal with them.

There can often be considerable delays in trying to get plans through the council and it is interesting to note that you are quite within your rights to give the proper notice for the building works to start on site without the plans actually being passed. The law does not state that your plans must be passed, but that the work carried out on site must conform to the Building Regulations.

Various other notices have to be given by the builders to the local authority if, for example, foundations are involved, or drainage. However, with loft conversions normally only a start notice is required and a completion notice when the works have been finished.

The local authority building control officer is entitled to come on site at any time he pleases – and so is the district surveyor and can make *ad hoc* inspections of the work to satisfy himself that it is proceeding in accordance with the regulations.

So that the structure shall be of sufficient strength and at the same time be economical in the use of materials, calculations to ensure that stresses and strains in the component parts of the building are not excessive are made by a consulting engineer.

This practice has become more widespread since reputable builders no longer rely on (and the local authority should not accept) rule-of-thumb methods to determine the size of various parts of a structure.

Calculations may be checked by the local authority who often employ structural engineers or retain the services of other consulting engineers to perform this function for them.

Like all rules and regulations laid down by Act of Parliament, regulations governing building works are complicated. They are also very lengthy. Your designer should know what he is doing with regard to the regulations and at least you have the comfort of knowing that he can and no doubt will be checked out by the local authority. The purpose of this chapter is to highlight the main regulations that affect the *concept* of your conversion at the initial planning stages.

As with income tax, avoidance may be practised but evasion may not. However, it is perhaps as well to remember that to evade income tax may end up burning a hole in your pocket, but to evade carrying out certain sensible building regulations may end up burning your house down!

ZONE OF OPEN SPACE
This rule is sometimes forgotten by designers of loft conversions and can be most embarrassing, to say the least, if the conversion is discovered as being in contravention once the building works have started.

In general terms this regulation requires the provision of a minimum zone of open space outside windows of habitable rooms. This space is defined by describing a theoretical upright shaft of space which must be open to the sky at the bottom and free from obstruction. It means that any new dormer window that is going to be within twelve ft (3·7 m) of the boundary is going to be suspect under this regulation in terms of the open zone of space outside it. The rule is a complicated one and needs studying carefully, so that if you find your property is very close to your neighbours and a habitable room is to be designed with a window on that side particular care must be taken. If the dormer is to cater only for a staircase then, of course, you will be all right.

FIRE RESISTANCE
In 1970 the sixth amendment to the Building Regulations was brought into force and this had an important effect on loft conversions. The regulations required that any house which has three or more storeys must have its staircase protected from the rest of the building. In a single family home this meant that the structure around the staircase had to be half-hour fire resistant. The walls around the staircase are usually half-hour fire resistant but the doors leading off the well of the stairs very often are not. Therefore, in converting the loft it means that the doors of the bedroom on the first floor and the living rooms and kitchen on the ground floor must be made half-hour fire resistant and self-closing.

Under the same regulation it is also necessary that the floor of the first floor is half-hour fire resistant – as well, of course, as the new loft conversion floor.

Fortunately, most local authorities allow relaxation of this regulation if the conversion is a small one. The rule-of-thumb guide is that if it is a single room then the doors leading off the staircase need only be made self-closing and the floor of the first floor need not be touched. If the new conversion has two rooms or more, then usually the full rigours of the law are imposed. This not only causes quite a performance in that carpets must be taken up so that flame proof boarding can be laid, but also the cost of changing or adjusting all the doors in the house for fire check doors is onerous indeed.

The fire regulations also insist that external walls are made of non-combustible material if they are within one metre (3 ft 3 ins) of the boundary. This rule is, of course, particularly significant for semi-detached and terraced houses since in effect it means that any dormer that has been designed into the roof slope must be kept in by three feet (91.4 cm), or else the external cladding must be non-combustible – or else you must build up the brickwork of the party wall.

Under the fire laws it is also deemed necessary to ensure that internal walls and ceilings are made with materials that minimize the spread of flame. However the regulation does not cover the surface decorating finish and so you may use whatever paint, wallpaper or fabric you like so long as the application does not form part of the actual structure. In other words if you are to build into the wall a particular timbered surface, for example, then that timber surface would have to be flame resistant (usually with a British Standard rating) for it to pass the regulations.

HABITABLE ROOMS

Any habitable room in the building has to be not less than 2.3 metres (7 ft 7 ins) in height. If the room is in the roof of the building there is a slight relaxation in that the height must not be less than 2.3 metres over an area of the floor of the room equal to not less than one half of the area of that room measured on a plane of 1.5 metres (4 ft 11 ins) above the floor. The regulation goes on to say that, for the purpose of the regulation, no account should be taken of the projection of any joist in the ceiling of a room. This means that if you cannot quite get the head room required then it is possible to produce what is known as a hollow joisted ceiling. This feature can in any case be quite attractive.

Habitable rooms also have to have adequate ventilation. The rule demands that the total area of ventilation is equal to not less than one twentieth of the floor area of that room and that some part of that area is not less than 1.75 metres (5 ft 9 ins) above the

floor. Oddly enough while a habitable room has to have ventilation there is no regulation that demands that it has to have natural light. However, under the London Building Act there is a demand that habitable rooms have light to the equivalent to one tenth of the floor area.

STAIRCASES

Because of the particular feature of staircases within loft conversions, the effects of this regulation has been covered in the chapter on design. However, it is enough to say that staircases do have to meet very critical requirements and it is important that this is fully assessed before going ahead with any scheme.

CHIMNEYS

Most houses have chimneys and they, too, are the subject of regulations. The prime rule that affects a loft conversion is that a chimney or flue must be one metre higher than the top of any opening window if that window is within 2.3 metres of the chimney itself. If the chimney is not in use, of course this does not apply but usually the local authority will insist that the chimney is either taken down or capped in case it is to be used at a later date.

Broadly speaking the same rule is made to apply for soil vent pipes – although the actual regulations merely state that the pipe be carried upwards to such a height and position 'as not to transmit foul air in such a manner as to become prejudicial to health or a nuisance'. Incidentally, it also insists that the top of a soil vent pipe has a durable wire cage or other cover which does not unduly restrict the flow of air.

PATIOS AND ROOF GARDENS

While it is pretty obvious that one has to take into account the various loads that are imposed on a new floor, it is most important that the weight of a patio or a roof garden is considered if it is to be incorporated into the conversion.

In general terms the structure of the building above the foundations must safely sustain and transmit to those foundations the combined load, imposed load and wind load without such deflection or deformation as will impair the stability of or cause damage to the whole or any part of the building. If you are going to grow a cherry tree in a tub on your patio you certainly don't want it ending up in your basement!

It is important to say that the onus of building under the Building Regulations is very much on you – the owner. The Building Regulations refer to the 'builder' as being the person being responsible for carrying out or intending to carry out any particular building operation, so that while you will rely on the firm of builders that you employ to do all this for you, if there is any contravention of the regulations as a last resort they will serve any notice on *you*, not them. Obviously, the local authority will get in touch with the firm of builders first as a matter of normal procedure because, of course, the building control officer will obviously be in touch with the building firm concerned.

There are many other regulations that have to be complied with, but the ones mentioned here are important at the initial stages of considering the conversion, both because of their impact on the technical side of design and also because of the cost implication. The Building Regulations and the London Building Acts are administered by competent and experienced men who put safety first. Your project is of prime importance to you, but your project is only one of thousands to the local authority. If, therefore, there is any conflict between you and the local authority you can be sure that it starts from that simple fact.

Chapter VI
Party walls

If you live in a detached house you can skip this chapter completely, but if you live in a semi-detached or terraced property then it is important that this chapter is understood. Before we go any further it is as well to say that this is an extremely boring subject but something which has to be covered.

Now, while it is very much in the wind that the planners would like to make the Inner London areas the same as the rest of the country, with regard to the aspect relating to adjoining owners, they would like the rest of the country to fall into line with the Inner London area. No doubt this is bad news from the point of view of a building owner, as will be seen while we wade through this particular chapter. In the Building Regulations areas there is no particular ruling with regard to party walls except for Common Law Rights, but within the Inner London area there are very definite rules and regulations which have been laid down by Act of Parliament and are still very much in force.

In the Outer London areas it is a matter of courtesy and common sense to let your neighbour know what you are doing and to ensure that the party wall is sufficient for the purposes for which you wish to use it. But this is not so in the Inner London area and this chapter is wholly devoted to this particular aspect.

The particular bit of buff paper to get hold of is published by Her Majesty's Stationery Office at the current price of 80p and is entitled, 'London Building Acts (Amendments) Act, 1930'.

You won't have to read all of this 150-page document but it is important that you read part VI all the way through. Mind you, you may find it fascinating to read part VIII which is entitled 'Sky Signs'. In that section you will find 'It shall be unlawful to erect a sky sign or to permit or suffer a sky sign to be erected or to obtain a sky sign'. However,

PARTY STRUCTURE NOTICE

To   Mr. G. Mitchell
of   22 Du Cane Road London N.W.3.
and to all whom it may concern.

As Building Owner(s) of the Premises known as 26 Du Cane
                                              Road, London N.W.3.

and with reference to the Party Structure separating
the said Premises from the adjoining Premises on the
East side thereof known as 22 Du Cane Road, London
N.W.3.

I hereby give you notice that after the expiration of
two months from the date of service hereof I intend
to exercise the rights given to me by the London
Building Acts (Amendment) Act, 1939, Section 46, by
carrying out the building works as stated below:-

        Carry out a loft conversion
        to my property in accordance
        with the drawings and
        specification attached to this
        document.

and I propose to commence the work on or about the
first day of April 1975.

I hereby appoint
Mr. G. Brown
of Atkinson, Horton and Partners, 2, Lower Fulham
                                  Road, London S.W.6.

to act as my Surveyor.   Building Owner
Signature   John Patterson
Address   26 Du Cane Road   London N.W.3.
Dated this   Eleventh day of January   1975

This is a typical Party Structure Notice which you have to serve on your next-door neighbour(s) two months before you can start building work.

Part VI is not quite so amusing and if your neighbour wants to be awkward and insists that the letter of the law be maintained, then it really does have a very particular significance for you.

In this section 'the foundation', 'party wall' and 'special foundations' are defined. It then goes on with the 'Rights and etc.', of owners, the differences between owners and the expenses.

Under Part VI of the Act the building owner has the right to carry out building works to his property even though it may involve the party wall that belongs jointly to him and to his adjoining neighbour. However, before he exercises any of the rights conferred upon him by the Act he is required to serve a notice on the adjoining owner in writing, stating the nature and particulars of the proposed work and a notice must be served at least two months before the date on which the work is to be done. This notice is known as 'a party structures notice', an example of which is on the left.

PARTY WALL AWARD

Once the party structures notice has been served on the adjoining owner, he has three alternative courses of action. First, he may give his simple consent within fourteen days of the notice having been served and that is the end of the matter. Or he may serve a 'counter notice' in which he may specify what he feels should be done with regard to the building works you are proposing to have done. Again, if he, or you (the building owner) cannot agree then a difference shall be deemed to have arisen between the two parties and it will be necessary for you to go through the whole performance of a Party Wall Award.

Once a difference has arisen either both parties shall concur in the appointment of one surveyor or each party shall appoint a surveyor each to act for them. If the latter course is taken then the two surveyor's shall also appoint a third surveyor to act as a referee. There are all sorts of complications that can arise with regard to one of the surveyors not carrying out the work, or an argument between the two surveyors or if the third surveyor dies or finally refuses to act, so it is important that you read carefully through section 55 of Part VI of the Act in order that you can fully understand what you might let yourself in for.

Generally speaking, each party appoints a surveyor and the two of them get together to assess the building works that the building owner proposes to carry out and they can then both agree on the state of the party wall as it exists and such damage or otherwise as is likely to be caused through the building works taking place. The result of all this is that an award is produced by the two surveyors and then work can proceed on the basis of the award which, if it has been properly drawn up, will fully protect the adjoining owner against any damage caused to his property and will also ensure that the building owner is safeguarded from the adjoining owner claiming all sorts of damage which was not part of the award.

Once the two surveyors have inspected both properties and, in particular, the state of the party wall, they then raise what is known as a Schedule of Conditions and this document is, in fact, a list of clauses designed to protect both parties from the consequences of the building works.

An example of the Schedule of Conditions forming part of the Party Wall Award, together with the Award document itself, is shown opposite.

These documents are typical of the Party Wall Award which you will have to arrange with your next-door neighbour(s). Part of the Award is a Schedule of Condition of the state of your neighbour(s)' property.

---

6. THAT   the works shall be carried
               reasonable expedition afte

7.. THAT   a signed copy of this Awar
               to the Adjoining Owner's S

8. THAT   the Building o

(b) THAT   the said wall is sufficient for the needs of the Adjoining Owner.

(c) THAT   the condition of the party wall an adjoining building is as described Schedule of Conditions attached he and forming part of this Award.

2. THAT   upon the signing hereof, the Buil Owner shall be at liberty to carr following works:-

AWARD IN THE MATTER OF
BUILDING ACTS (AMENDMEN
PART VI AND THE PARTY
SEPARATING THE PREMISES
26 DU CANE ROAD, LONDON
22 DU CANE ROAD, LONDON

WHEREAS   Mr. John Patterson of 26 Du (hereinafter referred to as Freeholder of the premises Road, London did on or abou January One thousand nine h five did serve upon Mr. G. referred to as the Adjoining the premises known as 22 Du adjoining Notice of his int rights given to him under t (Amendment) Act 1939 Sectio 1(a) (e) (f) (g) (j) and (k to the party wall between t more particularly defined i

AND WHEREAS   the Adjoining Owner having works within the time presc dispute is deemed to have a

AND WHEREAS   the Adjoining Owner has app of Malcolm Brooks and Assoc Putney S.W. to act as his S Building Owner has appointe Horton and Partners of 2, L London S.W.6. to act as his

AND WHEREAS   the two Surveyors so appoin Richard Darcy Esq., F.R.I.C and Company, 12 Queens Plac act as Third Surveyor in ac provisions of the Act or in being unable or unwilling t being unable to agree upon Surveyor to be appointed by the time being of the Royal Chartered Surveyors.

NOW WE   being two of the three Surv having inspected the said w
AND DETERMINE as follows:-

1. (a) THAT   the said wall dividing 26 LONDON N.W.3. on the East from 22 DU CANE ROAD, LOND deemed to be a party wall of the Act.

with
ement.

e furnished

N
39
—
ND

London N.W.3.
ing Owner)
6 Du Cane
day of
seventy
hereinafter
reeholder of
, London
exercise the
Building Acts
ub sections
ting works
ldings as
ce.

from the said
he Act, a

o Ross A.R.I.C.S.
h Street,
d the
of Atkinson,
n Road,

elected
id Edwards
S.W.1. to
ith the
of his
then
te, a
dent for
of

ppointed,
REBY AWARD

D,
f
s
meaning

FRONT ELEVATION

Brickwork in good condition.

Agreed between: Surveyor to Building Owner

and:

Conditions of the Party Wall between

22 and 26 Du Cane Road, London N. W. 3

on 16th February, 1975

Between: Theo Ross A.R.I.C.S. of
                            Malcolm Brooks & Associates Surveyor to
                            Adjoining Owner

and: Mr. G. Brown of Atkinson, Horton and
                            Partners Surveyor to Building Owner

The relevant visible portions of the party wall were inspected
in the two buildings and the condition was noted as follows:-

ROOF SPACE

Internal roof inspection revealed general decor poor.
Several cracks in plasterboard on party wall also signs
of dampness.

General condition of room appears to be in reasonable
condition.

External roof inspection to take place on commencement of
work.

SECOND FLOOR

Front Room: General plaster cracks around chimney breast
               in particular one diagonal crack in left alcove.
               Crack visible at the juncture of the party and
               partition wall. Ceiling paper appears to
               conceal several defects i.e. irregularities in
               ceiling. Damp patch visible in left alcove.

FIRST FLOOR

Front Room: Cracks visible at juncture of ceiling and party
               wall in both left and right hand alcove.

Chapter VII

Where to get it built

Apart from trying to do it yourself (which might be dangerous unless you are qualified) where do you go to get your conversion built? There are three different ways to tackle the problem – and none of them is foolproof. The most expensive way can end up being the cheapest because it all went without a hitch. On the other hand the cheapest can turn out to be the most expensive, because the whole thing started coming apart at the seams when finished. Life's like that.

There is a simple rule-of-thumb guide: you don't need an architect to design your conversion, but you do need a builder to build it.

ARCHITECT AND BUILDER

In the good old days when no one had to penny-pinch and everything was carried out in the proper way, you found an architect and commissioned him to produce all the designs and plans for whatever building works you had in mind. He drew up the specification and put it out to tender against an RIBA contract to three or four builders and then you accepted one of the quotations and your project got under way. You accepted the architect's fees (without question) and you paid the builder (with raised eyebrows) and that was that.

That, of course, was in the good old days when you didn't need a loft conversion in any case – you just moved house!

This is still a highly acceptable way of getting the job done. It is still the only way some people would approach it. The trouble these days, with galloping inflation and costs rising almost from day to day, is that the 'architect-client-builder' permutation tends to be a more costly, long-winded, affair. The result so often is an eternal triangle in which all parties wish they had not got involved in the first place. If this appears to be a cynical way of looking at the hitherto traditional method of getting the job done, why are there now two other ways of doing it, and are they any better?

LOFT CONVERSION SPECIALISTS

As the loft conversion market has increased, so too have the numbers of companies who carry out this work. Large or small, the companies may be classified under two distinct categories: companies specifically set up to carry out loft conversions *only*, and companies who carry out loft conversion *as well as* all other types of building work. The former will tend to advertise as 'Loft Conversion Specialists' and the latter as 'Specializing in Loft Conversions'.

The loft conversion specialists advertise in the national press and magazines and their glossy brochures would lead you to believe that they were the greatest. Certainly the commission salesman who will follow-up your inquiry will have a convincing tale to tell. Most of the companies offer a complete package from initial survey to the finished construction, and there is no doubt that they have some very satisfied customers as a result. In fact, the concept of what they have to offer is very good but here are two areas in which their approach can let you down.

In the main they offer a very fixed specification (to reduce costs?) and your individual preferences cannot always be properly attended to. For example, some offer a fixed range of windows, or a fixed style of skirting and architraves, or only fixed alternatives of staircase design. Most will not take on the many extra other building works you will want carried out as a result of the loft conversion taking place. You may want fitted cupboards built or, because of the reason for your loft conversion, you may require a garage to be built and that will mean calling in another firm of builders.

The second failing of the system stems from the fact that most of the specialist firms find it difficult to pick up enough business in their local area, and so expand their sales activities farther and farther afield, extending their lines of communication more and more. This often means that the site work becomes more remote from their base and sub-contractors have to be used – if, indeed, they are not used in any case.

Always ask the specialist companies this question: 'Do you have your own labour supervised on a day-to-day basis or do you use fixed price, labour-only, sub-contractors?' The answer could make all the difference to the way in which your project is handled.

BUILDERS WHO SPECIALIZE

The third method of getting your conversion carried out obviates the formal architect-builder approach and gives you the flexibility and personalization often missing from the specialist approach. This is where you find a competent local builder who specializes in loft conversions as well as carrying out general building work.

Many building companies have their own in-house design facilities and will be quite competent to produce the necessary plans for you. Those who do not have the in-house facility will certainly either have an associated facility in the shape of a surveyor or designer whom the firm uses regularly or be able to recommend an independent firm of designers in the area.

The building firm will be more than capable of originating the specification in accordance with your wishes and, of course, be only too pleased to take on any ancillary work that you may want to have done in or around your property at the same time.

Because the firm continually works in the area, it will of course be well known to the local authority and this will be helpful both in terms of getting the plans through and in liaison with building control.

The first method is not necessarily the best, but will probably be the most expensive. The second one has a lot of pitfalls even if you are lucky but it will very likely be the cheapest. The last way of setting about it requires good judgment in the choice of firm, but you will be most likely to get what you want at a middle price.

The difficulty has always been in finding the right firm. With the first method the architect will find you the builder. With the specialist firms their advertisements and salesmen will find you without too much trouble. But with the last method you have got to find them, since builders do very little to promote themselves.

Here are a few addresses of institutes and organizations that could help you:

Royal Institute of British Architects, 66, Portland Place, London W1N 3DH.

Royal Incorporation of Architects in Scotland, 15, Rutland Square, Edinburgh, EH1 2BE.

Royal Institute of Chartered Surveyors, 12, Great George Street, London SW1P 3AE.

Royal Institute of Chartered Surveyors, 7, Manor Place, Edinburgh, EH3 7DN.

The Loft Conversion Advisory Bureau, 600, Kingston Road, London, SW20 8DN.

The Building Centre, 26, Store Street, London WC1E 7BS.

The Design Centre, 28, Haymarket, London, SW1Y 4EN.

The Design Centre, 72, St. Vincent Street, Glasgow, G2 5TH.

Chapter VIII

Where to get the money

At the time of writing this chapter, the 'in' word in financial circles was *liquidity*. At first I thought that it meant that if you were as hard pressed over loot as the rest of us, and gave up and hit the bottle, you ended up by having a liquidity problem! However, I am assured that it is in fact related only to getting hold of money when you have bags of everything else instead and, I am further assured, it takes a sober mind to tackle the problem.

Your house is of course a major asset against which you can borrow provided that you have the wherewithall to pay it back. If your house is unencumbered then a straightforward building society loan may be arranged, normally over a 25-year term (post 1920) or a 20 year term (pre 1920) at an interest rate of around 11% to 11½%. If you already have an existing mortgage there are a number of alternatives:

1 Your existing building society may be prepared to increase your advance. This will normally mean adding to the outstanding balance with the period of the loan remaining unchanged and at the same interest rate.
2 You may be able to re-mortgage with another building society (i.e. redeem your existing mortgage) and effect a new loan for your present loan *plus* the cost of the conversion over an equivalent term.
3 You can obtain a second mortgage (i.e. retain your existing) and go to an alternative source for the cost of the conversion.

The first two options are pretty straightforward but the third has quite a number permutations of which the following are the more common:

1 You can approach an insurance company for a loan, which will normally be until the conclusion of the first mortgage, repaid by an endowment policy with the interest rate probably fixed at between 11% and 13%.
2 Your bank manager could give you a loan for 3 to 5 years at an interest rate of at least 3% over their base rate. The capital is usually repaid in level amounts over the period.
3 Merchant banks, secondary banks and finance houses will all give loans over 2–10 years (sometimes 15 years) with an interest rate of at least 18% and possibly linked to bank base rate. Repayment is normally in level amounts over the period.

There are two other reasonable sources of finance which are worth looking at:

1 An endowment or whole life policy that you have been paying into for a number of years may well have a substantial loan value. The interest rate will be around 11% and the loan will remain outstanding until maturity date of the policy or when ever you chose to repay it.
2 Solicitors often have access to Trust Fund money and they may lend it to generate income, subject to necessary safeguards.

All the lending sources mentioned may require to survey the property. Building societies charge a scale survey fee based on the value of the property. Second mortgage firms charge a valuation fee – this is usually less than the scale survey fee – and all bank loans are normally subject to a committment fee of ½% to 1% of the advance.

Early redemption of a loan may require the borrower to pay a penalty of up to six months interest, although some sources may accept notice of intention to redeem in lieu.

Tax relief at the borrower's marginal rate is available on interest paid in respect of loans for loft conversions provided that the property is owner occupied and the total loan(s) not in excess of £25,000.

You may be rash enough to think 'What about a grant – surely the Government must be doing something to encourage people to stay put because of the housing shortage?' The short answer is 'No'. The Housing Act 1974 encourages you to produce an additional home for someone else but not for you or your own.

If your conversion is for your expanding family or for your grandmother, mother-in-law, or any other worthy person to occupy as part of your home, they won't play ball. Improvement grants only go to the owner occupier who provides a self-contained unit available for letting.

To provide such accommodation you first need planning permission for change of use from 'single dwelling' to 'multi-occupation' and you must meet all the stringent fire regulations and ensure that the conversion is completely self-contained. Depending on the area, your house may have to have a rateable value of less than £175 and you have got to have let the new unit within five years after completion, or you have to pay the grant back – plus compound interest!

If you can meet all those and a few other conditions as well, you may qualify, depending on where you live, for a grant of 50%, or 60% or even 70% of the eligible expense up to £3,200.

So you see, the short answer really is 'No' – but even if you do want to achieve a self contained flat and go for a grant, the chances are that by the time you have waded through all the red tape the building cost will have gone up by as much as the grant anyway. Square one!

To end on that word 'liquidity': remember that the money market is a pretty liquid place with quite a lot of sharks swimming about in it. So take care and try to get advice from a qualified friend. Some of these addresses might help you:

Building Society Association, 14, Park Street, London W1Y 3WD.

*British Insurance Association, Aldermary House, Queen Street, London, EC4P 4JD.

Life Officers Association, Aldermary House, Queen Street, London, EC4N 11P.

*Corporation of Insurance Brokers, 15; St. Helens Place, London EC3A 6DE.

Corporation of Mortgage and Finance Brokers 34, Rose Street, Wokingham, Berkshire RG11 1XU.

Committee of London Clearing Bankers, 10, Lombard Street, London EC3N 9AP.

Committee of Scottish Clearing Bankers, 19, Rutland Square, Edinburgh EH1 2DD.

Corporation of Mortgage & Finance Brokers, 140, Hope Street, Glasgow G2 2TG.

*You are advised to apply to the London offices of the British Insurance Association and the Corporation of Insurance Brokers for the names and addresses of regional officers.

Summary data sheet

Now that you have read this book, I hope that you will be able to go quite a long way towards producing a basic lay-out of your loft conversion. While you obviously need expert advice with regard to the structural detail, you will certainly have your own thoughts on what you hope it will look like. To help you formulate your ideas, you may find this data sheet of some value when the time comes to discuss the design and originate the specification.

Type of house

Whether your house is
☐ detached
☐ semi-detached
☐ terraced
☐ bungalow
Try and identify its overall appearance and add on any extensions, bonnets, etc., as per the roof plan below.

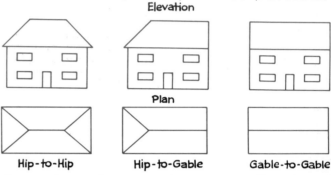

Elevation

Plan

Hip-to-Hip   Hip-to-Gable   Gable-to-Gable

If your house has a much more complicated roof structure you may have to leave it until your designer has seen it. In most cases, if you measure the length and breadth of the loft at a height of 3 feet 6 inches (1·07 metres) off the ceiling joists, you will ascertain the approximate dimensions of the floor area (indicated by the broken line on the plan above).

Planning permission

Unless your house or the locality is subject to a special order, you will not need planning permission if:
☐ Your conversion does not exceed the height of the original house.
☐ It does not come in front of the forwardmost part of the building.
☐ It does not exceed, together with any other addition to the property, 1,765 cubic feet (50 cubic metres) or ten per cent of the cubic area up to a maximum of 1,061 cubic feet (115 cubic metres).
The existing ridge height must be able to allow a finished floor-to-ceiling height of 7 feet 7 inches (2·3 metres) to produce a habitable room.

Roof, dormers and windows

Existing roof:
☐ slate
☐ tile
☐ colour and condition
☐ insulation
Dormers. You will need expert advice on size and positioning, but consider the following:
☐ cheeks to match or contrast

Ridge Height.

Dormer addition to the front, rear or side up to 50 cubic meters. (65·4 cubic yards)

Ground extensions to the rear or side, only up to 50 cubic meters (65·4 cubic yards)

☐ roof asphalted, or felt and chippings, or p.v.c. type
☐ fascias, gutters and flashings
☐ effect of soil vent pipe and chimneys
☐ balcony, window boxes, etc.
Windows:
☐ timber, metal or aluminium
☐ casement, sliding or other
☐ single or double glazed
☐ roof lights
☐ window catches, child-proof locks, etc.

Staircase

You will need expert advice on the positioning of the staircase, but the appearance is important if it is to blend in. Consider the following:
☐ open tread (hardwood?)
☐ box tread (softwood?)
☐ cut strings
☐ style of baluster
☐ type of handrail
☐ appearance of newels
☐ finish

Rooms and fire resistance

With a single room you should obtain relaxation over the fire regulations. With two rooms or more you will need to check the possibility of:
☐ fire check doors on habitable rooms leading off the stairs
☐ flame-proof boarding covering the first floor

Plumbing

If the water tanks must be repositioned:
☐ check condition of existing tank
If extension of central heating:
☐ check efficiency of boiler
☐ consider hot water method for basin and bath
☐ position of existing soil pipe for lavatory
☐ check headroom for shower and efficiency of water feed

Electrics

You will probably need a new ring main for the conversion, but what is your existing wiring like? Always have ample electrical points, they are expensive to add later. Consider the number of:
☐ power points (13 amp) single or double (switched?)
☐ pendant lights
☐ wall and spot lights
☐ strip lights (with shaver socket?)
☐ light of storage area
☐ two-way over stairs
☐ t.v. aerial
☐ night storage (white meter)

Finish and fittings

External:
☐ Painting done as part of contract because of accessibility.
☐ Do you need other maintenance done to the property while men on site?
Internal:
☐ plastered finish
☐ style of architraves and skirting
☐ door furniture and locks
☐ bathroom fittings and vanity units
☐ fitted cupboards
☐ ceiling coving
☐ decorating

Additional work

While you are going to have builders on site, is there other work that needs to be done?
☐ first floor
☐ ground floor
☐ kitchen
☐ porch
☐ car port
☐ patio
☐ garden wall

If loft conversion is impracticable what about a ground extension as an alternative?